JIM CORBETT OF KUMAON

JIM CORBETT OF KUMAON

JIM CORBETT
OF
KUMAON

D.C. KALA

RAVI DAYAL Publisher
Delhi

Published by
RAVI DAYAL Publisher
51 E Sujan Singh Park
New Delhi 110003

Distributed by
ORIENT LONGMAN LTD
Bangalore Bhubaneshwar Calcutta Chennai
Ernakulam Guwahati Hyderabad Lucknow
Mumbai New Delhi Patna

First published 1979
This revised edition published 1999

ISBN 81 7530 022 1

Typeset by Rastrixi, New Delhi 110070
Printed at Rekha Printers Pvt. Ltd., New Delhi 110020.

To Padma with love

Preface to the First Edition

THIS BOOK is for Corbett fans in repayment of a debt India owes the hunter. Unashamedly, I must admit a lot of it is Corbett rewritten. All his six available books of the seven he wrote have been screened for biographical material. But there are new facts as well over and above the ones provided by Corbett himself and his three earlier biographers: Marjorie Clough, Director of the American Red Cross at Agra during World War II, who provided material to *Current Biography* (1946 edition); Lord Hailey, a former Governor of the United Provinces (modern Uttar Pradesh) who wrote the introduction to *Tree Tops*, Corbett's last book (1955); and Geoffrey Cumberlege of Oxford University Press, London, who wrote the introduction to the World's Classics edition of *Man-Eaters of Kumaon* and *The Temple Tiger* (1960).

Cumberlege's is the best account based on a close study of Corbettiana and long talks with Corbett's sister Maggie. Marjorie Clough worked for the American National Red Cross till 1947 but my efforts to contact her at her last known address proved unsuccessful. Cumberlege also could not be contacted, and Hailey is dead.

In April 1971, while I was holidaying at Bhim Tal, someone pointed out to me Corbett's fishing lodge overlooking the dam-end of the lake. A talk with its former keeper's son, Chatur Singh, then gardener in the Canal Department there, led to some ideas. At Naini Tal, looking for material, I met two sons of his Indian friends who provided interesting guidelines. Then I called at the district record room, the registrar's office, the public library and the municipal board office and struck luck. I also met all the resident Whites and near-Whites of the area and his former tenants of the Kaladhungi village, Choti Haldwani.

The end result I must say is far from satisfactory because of the grudging response from government departments which were approached to dig up old records. But from the kind people of Naini Tal I received enormous cooperation. Without it even this attempt, a base perhaps for a more resourceful biographer some day, would not have been possible.

Some two hundred letters went out to check on facts. The response was fair. One led to a trip to Bombay to meet R.E. Hawkins, former General Manager of Oxford University Press, India, who was kind enough to lead me on to earlier material and provided new facts.

The reader may note that the names of some places, trees, birds and animals have been spelled differently from Corbett's spellings. These are the correct spellings, for this biographer too has spent half his life in Kumaon. But I have retained Corbett's own spellings wherever I have quoted him.

Quotations taken from Corbett's books and referred to in the footnotes are from *Man-Eaters of Kumaon*, Peacock book, Penguin Books Ltd., 1970; *The Man-Eating Leopard of Rudraprayag*, Oxford University Press, 1948; *My India*, Oxford University Press (Champak Library edition), 1968; *Jungle Lore*, Oxford University Press, 1953; *The Temple Tiger*, Oxford University Press, 1965; and *Tree Tops*, Oxford University Press, 1955.

New Delhi
February 1979

D.C. KALA

Acknowledgements

THE AUTHOR gratefully acknowledges the kindness of the following who made this book possible:

The Oxford University Press for allowing him to quote extensively from the six Corbett books published by them and their two journals; Ruby Beyts for the use of thirteen pages of unpublished notes dictated by Corbett's sister, Maggie, to her; R.E. Hawkins and Donald Eichert for reading the manuscript of the first edition, and Ravi Dayal for helping revise the text for the second; Eric Sherbrooke Walker for the photograph of Corbett with birds; Col. E.H. Newington for the photograph of Corbett's grave; F. Valla for the photograph of the old Tree Tops; Henry Z. Walck for information on the launching of *Man-Eaters of Kumaon* in the United States; Gita Ram for the photograph of Gulab Rai; N. Thiagarajan for the Kaladhungi photographs; the Forest Department of Uttar Pradesh for permission to photograph exhibits inside the Corbett museum; G.M. Hopkins and W.H. Baldwin for allowing him to quote their letters; the Keeper of India Office Records for information on the early Corbetts; his friend the late Hira Lal Sah, librarian at the Municipal Board Library, Naini Tal, for the *Review of the Week*; Devi Lal Sah, Aloke Sah and M.M. Kholia of Naini Tal for pursuing the town inquiries; N.R. Smith for digging up records of the uprising in 1857; V.C. Bhaskaran for research; and his father G.R. Kala, author of *Memoirs of the Raj*, for sharing his first-hand knowledge of the life and times of Jim Corbett.

Contents

List of Plates

(between pp. 84 and 85)

1 The Story

THE SETTING of this book is two continents—Asia, which raised Lieutenant-Colonel Edward James Corbett, IARO, VD, OBE, CIE,[1] Kaisar-i-Hind; and Africa, which gathered him to its arms in death. His triumphs were distributed between two countries, India and Kenya. Except for the last seven years of his life, he lived in India, a tiger among men, lover of the underdog, a hero in war and pestilence, a model zamindar and employer, an ascetic, naturalist, and, above all, a hunter of maneating tigers and leopards for thirty-two active years in the then three hill districts of Uttar Pradesh comprising Garwhal, Naini Tal and Almora. Others hunted, but he also wrote. Of his seven books *Man-Eaters of Kumaon*, a breathless whirl through tigerland, got him millions of fans and a top niche as a narrator of true jungle stories. In the realm of high adventure, he is a man of the five continents where his fans are and will be.

Except for a lone triumph, Africa was a continent of sorrow for him. He stayed there, dogged by ill-health, as a refugee after the exit of the British Raj from India, unsure of the changing times, the White sahib looking for another colony. True, his two closest relations were there and also his friends —we shall come to them later. The hero's exit from the Indian scene was silent. None of his tenants knew their landlord was going, nor did the hundreds of poor Whites and

---

[1] Indian Army Reserve of Officers (IARO); VD, a decoration for voluntary officers; Officer of the Order of the British Empire (OBE); Companion of the Indian Empire (CIE).

near-Whites who stayed behind in Kumaon. The secret was let out only to a few friends.

Corbett was admired in his home town, Naini Tal, an unassuming man greeting high and low, exuding bonhomie. As a city father for no less than twenty-eight years, he is well remembered for keeping the forested area of the town intact from vandals. His tenants adored him. And all over the hill districts of Kumaon the legend of the hunter lives on in a dozen folk songs and a thousand tales of 'Carpet' Sahib. The Prime Minister-to-be of the province, G.B. Pant, was a crony of his with whom he spent hours (whenever Pant was in town and out of prison), swapping yarns of the Tarai, where both had worked and lived. He was the only Congressman Corbett liked. At least in one land deal he was Corbett's lawyer too.

Corbett's heart was always in Kumaon, in the village of Kaladhungi where he had his winter home, and in Naini Tal, high up fifteen miles away, where he lived in summer. 'I'd like to be reborn in Kumaon', he would often say. Ensconced in the Baden-Powell cottage of the Outspan Hotel, Nyeri, off the Aberdare National Park in the Kenya Highlands, he sat worrying about his former tenants—he had freed them when he left—giving advice to a friend suffering from beri-beri, sending a fountain pen to a friend's son on his passing the Bachelor of Arts examination, wanting to take back the house (now the Corbett museum) he sold at Kaladhungi for the benefit of his tenants and dutifully sending till the end the land rent of Rs 910 a year on behalf of his tenants to the government.

From Kenya, he swapped notes with E.P. Gee, a brother naturalist (*Wild Life of India*), on the tigers of Hailey National Park, which Gee visited in 1954. And he compared notes with his friends in India on the Mau Mau and the Indian freedom movement. He was spared the indignity of seeing the exit of the Raj from Kenya though. Kenya became free in 1963 after sixty-eight years of White rule. Corbett died on 19 April 1955. But his sister, Margaret Winifred Corbett, who stuck to him till the end, saw the exodus.

India remembered Corbett by renaming its first national park after him in 1957. This was Hailey National Park, set up in 1935. In the first flush of freedom, while the tide of nationalism crested, it was found necessary to erase the memory of the builders of the Raj, and the Park was harmlessly renamed the Ramganga National Park in 1955 after the river which formed its northern boundary. The government would have perhaps immortalized Corbett's friend, who became the prime minister of U.P., but Pant stepped aside and helped in renaming it after Corbett.

I am sure Corbett would have been embarrassed to take over the Park, once named after Malcolm Hailey, Governor of the United Provinces in 1928–30 and 1931–34, a friend of his and a keen conservationist. Hailey outlived Corbett by at least fifteen years. Corbett was dead when the renaming came. And what could be a more fitting memorial than a tract of 324 square kilometres (now 528.8) in the Himalayan foothills for the tiger to survive in, I hope forever? Pant too got several memorials, including the renaming of the Ramsay Hospital at Naini Tal after him. This was the great Henry Ramsay who came to Kumaon in 1837 and ruled it for twenty-eight years as its sixth Commissioner. An early builder of the Raj, he was responsible for hundreds of projects and a thousand good deeds.

Corbett and his Premier friend, two of Naini Tal's best-known sons, share 1,000 square yards of land on the Flats, as the upper end of the lake is known. Pant stands on a pedestal. His statue is black and larger than life. Corbett stands by the water unobtrusively and unknown in the form of a bandstand for which he donated Rs 7,300 in 1919 for the 'benefit of Naini Tal'. The hunter and angler is where the water is. The politician has his back on half the town and faces the other half where the road begins down-hill to the dusty plains. Few know the history of the bandstand, but Gurney House on Ayarpata Hill, which Corbett's sister Margaret Winifred (Maggie) inherited from her mother, is well known. He lived in this house before he left for Kenya. A third son of Naini Tal who left his mark but no monument was Gen. Orde Charles Wingate, the Chindit, who died in an air crash in Burma in 1944.

The 'Corbett museum' at his village of Choti Haldwani, near Kaladhungi, came later, a pitiable effort of the state Forest Department to perpetuate the hunter's memory by displaying some photographs and letters he wrote to Indian friends. This too was done in the Premier's days. The odds and ends displayed there are what the villagers have not rifled from the untenanted house. The government acquired the house, restored it and set up the museum. Our man was generous with his minor trophies, and the Forest Department has not been able to collect the major ones, for these were auctioned by the executors of his will in Nairobi and are scattered all over the globe.

World recognition from brother naturalists came in 1968 with the naming of a subspecies of tiger after Corbett. This is *Panthera tigris corbetti*, found in Indo-China and extreme South China. It is slightly shorter than the Indian tiger and characterized by a 'darker ground coloration and more numerous, rather short, narrow and rarely doubled stripes'. It was named after Corbett by Dr Vratislav Mazak to honour the 'excellent naturalist who devoted his life to the study and the protection of Indian wild-life, particularly the tigers'.[2]

I spoke earlier of a personal triumph of Corbett's in Africa. That came in 1952, a few years before his death. He was privileged to escort Princess Elizabeth, who later ascended the British throne as Queen Elizabeth II, to Tree Tops Hotel in the Aberdare Mountains, near Nyeri, on a sightseeing safari a day before her father's death. Right from 1919, when he finished with the railways and practically retired to be a gentleman of leisure and businessman, ending up with a considerable fortune by the prevailing standards, he was in the foothill forests every winter with governors, collectors and

[2] *Extrait de Mammalia*, Tome 32, No. 1.

at least one viceroy, hobnobbing with them, gun or fishing rod in hand.

Every collector of the district or the forest officer who shot and fished became a friend. So did the maharajas, Jind for one. Young White rookies posted to the district turned to him for their first lessons in tiger hunting. Because of his association with the top district officers he commanded considerable influence in the area. A Corbett complaint was always heard. To Kaladhungi he had a museum approach. He wanted it unspoiled, with himself as patriarch to whom all could turn for help.

Born on 25 July 1875, Corbett spent his childhood at Kaladhungi and Naini Tal. He was educated at Naini Tal. After school, he went straight to Bihar to work on the railways for twenty-three years. In 1914, when World War I broke out, he returned to Kumaon to raise a labour contingent for the British Army and served in France and Waziristan. After World War I, he settled down at Naini Tal, where he lived almost continuously till 1947, except for several trips to Tanganyika (modern Tanzania) and a stint during World War II training Allied troops in jungle war as a Lieutenant-Colonel. As a city father of Naini Tal, he stepped into his father's shoes. The rest of the time he kept watch on all the bad tigers and leopards of the high hills and the adjoining plains.

These big, bad cats, maneaters to be precise, were Corbett's extra charge. When one was proclaimed a maneater by the district authorities, they turned to him for help to rid them of it. Sometimes the call came from the stricken villagers themselves. Several requests even reached Mokameh Ghat, Bihar, where he worked during his railway days. He always agreed. Tracking and killing maneaters needs considerable skill and daring. The maneating leopard of Rudraprayag he killed was responsible for the death of 125 persons in a reign of terror of eight years in northern Garhwal. Another less-publicized leopard, the maneater of Panar, took 400 human lives.

When the call came, the 40-pound tent, the suitcase and the bedroll were hurriedly packed by sister Maggie, the porters were collected, and the hunter set out in forced marches of twenty to forty miles a day—depending on the urgency—to the dak bungalow nearest to the last reported kill. Often, even after the last day's long march, he denied himself rest, left kit and porters at the dak bungalow and made a beeline to the kill or checked the lay of the land. If the kill was fresh enough, he would select a tree overlooking it, seek out a fork or comfortable branch and spend the night in it waiting for a shot at the marauder.

For weeks and sometimes months the strenuous hunt would go on in high tension up the hills and down the valleys as each new kill was reported, for every day gone meant more lives lost. Breakfasts, lunches and dinners were skipped. A maneating tiger or leopard acquires a special cunning by its long association with humanity. It loses all fear, finding the biped the most defenceless creature in nature's kingdom. When this happens, the hunter is also the hunted and gives himself at best a 50 : 50 chance in spite of his shooting iron. Corbett himself admits: 'There is no more terrible thing than to live and have one's being under the shadow of a maneater.'[3]

[3] *Man-Eaters of Kumaon*, p. 29.

2 *The Corbetts*

C ORBETT WAS inordinately proud of the fact that his family had lived in India for a long period. The Corbetts were of Irish stock. Grandfather Joseph Corbett, born at St Peter's, Dublin, left his native island for Bengal aboard the *Royal George*, a sailing vessel, on 26 July 1814. A carver and gilder by profession, he had enlisted for unlimited service as a private in the infantry on 15 June the same year, when eighteen. He arrived in India on 7 February 1815 with his wife Harriet and twelve-month-old daughter, Eliza. It took at least six months to reach India by the Cape of Good Hope route.

Joseph was transferred to the artillery in 1817, where he continued till his death at thirty-three on 28 March 1830. He is buried at Meerut. At the time of his death he was a sergeant in the horse artillery. The India Office records provide the following biodata on him: Visage/long; hair/black; eyes/hazel; complexion/sallow; height 5 feet 4 inches.

Christopher William, Jim's father, was born at Meerut on 11 September 1822, the third child of Joseph and Harriet. Joseph had by then risen to the rank of Corporal in the Horse Battery. Christopher was seven when his father died. The other children were John (born 1818), Catherine (1820), Richard Henry (1824), Harriet (1827) and Thomas Bartholomew (1828). The last of them was tied to a tree and burnt alive by insurgents during the siege of Delhi in 1857. Christopher William also took part in the fighting in Delhi.

Christopher William next surfaces at Mussoorie, the hill station overlooking Dehra Dun. He married Mary Anne

Morrow, aged eighteen, at Landour, then a suburb of Mussoorie, on 19 December 1845. His rank is given in the marriage register as assistant apothecary.

'Apothecary' was an army rank equivalent to assistant surgeon. Apothecaries were later designated apothecary lieutenants, and apothecary captains on promotion. The term was also loosely applied to chemists as well as to all those practising Western medicine.

We do not know where Christopher William was educated or apprenticed. But he was a doctor, and considering his fighting record I should like to think he was an army doctor. Landour was a cantonment station too. December is a rather cold month for a Mussoorie marriage. It looks as if Christopher William was a permanent resident of the station and not a transient summer visitor. He had three children from Mary Anne, two sons and one daughter, before she died. Fourteen years after his first marriage we find Christopher marrying again. On 13 October 1859 he married Mary Jane Doyle at Landour. She was the daughter of John and Mary Olive Prussia and the widow of Charles James Doyle of Agra, also a doctor. Christopher William was now a full-fledged apothecary.

The Prussias had three children—two sons and a daughter. John Prussia died while still quite young, leaving his wife to bring up the children. When the boys were old enough to go to school, Mary Olive Prussia decided to join her brother at Ferozepore, in Punjab, taking with her the little girl, Mary Jane. There were no railways at that time, and travelling was done by bullock cart and country boat. Undaunted, the two started off on a journey of many hundreds of miles [from Calcutta] without an escort, and after some months arrived safely at their destination where they were warmly welcomed by the brother and his family.[1]

In 'Recollections of Jim Corbett', dictated by Maggie and called Ruby Beyts' notes in this book, Maggie has studiedly remained silent on her grandfather from the father's side.

[1] Ruby Beyts' notes.

Apparently a mere gunner for a grandfather was not much to talk about.

Mary Jane was born in Calcutta on 12 March 1837 and baptized at St Andrew's Church there on 10 July. John Prussia was an employee of the Ishapore gun carriage factory first and then of the Serampore paper mills. Mary Jane married Doyle at Ferozepore when she was fourteen and Doyle twenty-one. The Doyles moved on to Agra. She had four children from him, two sons and two daughters. One of the daughters died of smallpox in infancy. This daughter, Evangelene, is buried in the Tota Talao cemetery in Agra. The grave is close to the cemetery gate. The other children were Charles, George and Eugene Mary. When the Mutiny broke out, the mother and children were sent to the fort for safety, along with the other Whites at Agra. Charles Doyle joined the local levies to fight the mutineers. The mother and the children suffered much in the siege. With the death of Doyle in the battle of Harchand-pore in the winter of 1858 Mary Jane found herself a widow at twenty-one, with a small pension and friendless. She went to Mussoorie with her three children after the death of her husband. There she met Christopher and married him within a year. They are both referred to as residents of Landour in the marriage register.

Doyle, who died when twenty-nine, is buried in the cemetery at Etawah. He died on 8 December 1858. 'The engagement of Harchandpore occurred about a month after the district was supposed to be pacified. A body of Oudh mutineers entered Etawah and plundered indiscriminately. They were severely defeated by the local levies: Mr Doyle (he was a volunteer civilian, not a soldier) was in command of the cavalry, consisting of the Etawah Light Horse, and the 13th Troop of Police Cavalry. After killing two men he was dismounted and cut to pieces.'[2]

The Etawah church also has a tablet reading: 'Sacred to the memory of Charles James Doyle, who fell leading a small

[2] *Mutiny Narratives of NWP, 1857–1858.*

band against overwhelming numbers of savage foes at the battle of Harchandpore . . . truehearted, generous and gentle as he was brave. His companions in arms have erected this tablet in remembrance of their lost friend; fighting only in his country's cause, beloved and respected by all his comrades and at peace with God.'[3] Allen O. Hume, then the collector of Etawah and later the founder of the Indian National Congress, was in overall command.

In 1862, after having spent the first two years of his married life in Muttra and Mussoorie, Father [Christopher William], who had joined the postal service after the Mutiny, was transferred to Naini Tal. As there was no train service, the journey from Mussoorie to Naini Tal had to be made by doolie dak. A doolie was a large boxlike contrivance suspended from poles and capable of accommodating a number of people. This conveyance was carried on the shoulders of eight stalwart doolie bearers. Travelling by day as well as by night along a road which ran for many miles through dense jungles teeming with wild life, the journey was not accomplished without its thrills. Sometimes the doolie had to be put down because of a tiger on the road, while strips would be torn from a bedsheet, soaked in kerosene oil, and used as flares to frighten the tiger away. The doolie would then continue on its journey. On arrival at Kaladhungi, in the foothills of the Himalayas . . . the mode of travel was changed from the doolie to the dandy, a sort of hammock, composed of a durrie (a small cotton carpet) attached to a pole. This was placed on the ground and when the occupant was comfortably (?) settled in, and keeping uneasily in position by holding on to the pole, the journey was begun. It is hard to imagine a more uncomfortable method of travelling. Only the women and children resorted to it.[4]

Christopher William Corbett, a veteran of the First Afghan War, the Sikh wars of the 1840s (with medals from the battles of Sobraon, Aliwal and Chilianwala) and the Mutiny, now starts with a family of six children in 1859—the three Doyle

[3] E.A.H. Blunt, *Christian Tombs and Monuments in the United Provinces*, 1911, p. 94.

[4] Ruby Beyts' notes.

children and three of his own.[5] In the course of the next few years he raised a substantial family of nine more—six sons and three daughters—from Mary Jane. The eldest of these was Tom (Thomas Bartholomew), named after the Mutiny hero; he was Jim Corbett's childhood idol and worked in the post office at Naini Tal where he was postmaster in 1855. In the Naini Tal Municipal Board records there is a letter drawing the attention of the postmaster to the insanitary state of the post office compound.

In 1794, twenty years before Joseph Corbett set sail for India, a Nestor of Limerick, Ireland, left for India aboard the *William Pitt*. A son, William Richard Nestor, in the employ of the East India Company, married Harriet Mary Dwyer in the Garrison Church of Calcutta, now no longer standing, six years before the Mutiny. After the Mutiny, William Richard was transferred to the secretariat of the North-West Province (later United Provinces of Agra and Oudh). His winter headquarters were at Allahabad, and the summer was spent at Naini Tal.

According to the Rev. A.W.T. Nestor, formerly of Agra and a grandson of William Richard, the latter bought land in Kaladhungi after the Mutiny. But he lost it in paying the debts of a friend for whom he had generously stood surety. William Richard died in 1880. The Nestors could be the second family of Whites in Kaladhungi which Jim Corbett mentions in *Jungle Lore*. There were also some Morrisons. In the Kaladhungi land records there is only a bare mention of them, as people owning land.

There is a town tradition too of a Morrison ghost being often seen at the Baur river bridge—Corbett spells it as Boar—a man dressed in immaculate white. The Nestors provided a bride to a Corbett and the Corbetts one to a Nestor. The Nestors too were a fecund family with thirteen children, alternately girl and boy, seven girls and six boys.

[5] According to Cumberlege, there were three children, Ruby Beyts' notes say two.

On his transfer to Naini Tal, postmaster Christopher Corbett secured a grant of land in the village of Choti Haldwani at Kaladhungi from Ramsay, the Commissioner, who thought it would be a good idea if the family had a winter retreat away from the severe weather at Naini Tal. Kaladhungi, which literally means 'black rock' in Kumaoni, the hill dialect, had nothing much to offer in the 1860s to a White man when the grant was made. It is at the base of the hills, below Naini Tal, the picturesque 6,000-foot-high hill station with a bowl-like lake.

Kaladhungi is sultry for six months in the year. The town is still surrounded by dense forest, and before the advent of DDT and the World Health Organization, which curbed malaria, it was well known as the hill man's graveyard. But the town was the centre of a thriving iron industry, based on local ore and forest charcoal, run by Davis and Company. After its merger with Drummond and Company, the North of India Kumaon Iron Works Company operated it till its closure in 1864. The town was the terminus of the dak-gharry service which operated on the trunk route connecting Moradabad and Naini Tal before the Bareilly-Kathgodam road and its extension to the Brewery opened a new route to the hill station in 1891.

The iron works and the hotel in Kaladhungi—two buildings of the Murray Hotel stand opposite the Jim Corbett estate and are still intact—must have been the only two things providing sustenance to a White man there. But Christopher was not in Kaladhungi doing a job. He built a house there only to escape Naini Tal's bitter winter. The ruins of Christopher's house, which stand by the Baur canal, face south. This house, named Arundel, has been in ruins for the past seventy-five years. The house figures in Corbett's childhood memories. Jim's own house, now the museum, was built or renovated by Jim himself later on land he bought from a local resident. The land with Arundel, just ten acres, was not big enough for profitable farming. Christopher only planted an orchard there with a variety of fruit trees. He was a keen gardener, but not a grand plantation owner.

Building materials were easy to find—stone from the nearby river beds, bricks burnt on the spot, and timber from the adjoining forest. Labour also was available and cheap, all the building along the foothills being done by the artisans from the hills who had come down to the low country to escape the cold. These people were known as the ghamtappas (sun-baskers) and formed the greater part of the winter foothill population. The house, consisting of a big living room with bedrooms opening off it, and surrounded on three sides by a big verandah, became the winter home from the time of its completion. It stood on high ground in a lovely setting of bamboos and big trees.[6]

At the time of the Mutiny the trunk road from Moradabad to Naini Tal saw much traffic in White men and women fleeing to the hills to find a haven. From Lucknow then, by this route, 'the hills were six days away for married people and four for bachelors'. The dak-gharry stages from Moradabad, the railhead, to Naini Tal were Rampur, Bazpur, Garappu and Choti Haldwani. The gharry was abandoned at Choti Haldwani where the travellers, after an overnight stay at Murray Hotel, negotiated the fifteen-mile climb to Naini Tal on horses or in dandies.

The birth register of St John-in-the-Wilderness, Naini Tal's oldest church, records the birth of Christopher William's third child from his second marriage in 1864. The first two, Thomas and Harriet, were born either at Mussoorie or at Mathura. The last seven children born in Naini Tal were Christopher Edward (1864), John Quinton (1867), Edith (1869), Maurice (1871), Margaret Winifred (1874), Edward James (1875) and Archibald D'Arcy (1879). In all, there were six boys and three girls.

Thomas Bartholomew married Emily Harriet and had a son from her in 1888. This was Lieut.-Gen. Thomas William Corbett, formerly of the Indian Army, who ran a farm with Jim Corbett and Brig. G.H.B. Beyts, also formerly of the Indian Army, at Mweiga, in Kenya. Both eventually settled in Britain. Christopher Edward was the manager of Albion

[6] Ruby Beyts' notes.

Hotel, Naini Tal, and was later an assistant in Murray and Company. He married Helen Mary Nestor. Harriet married Dick Nestor of the UP Civil Service. Edith married a Haslett. The Doyles did better.

Having been married for seven years and deeply devoted to her husband [Doyle], Mother was now left with a small widow's pension and three children to educate, but owing to her husband having taken out a life insurance policy she was able to use this money later on to send Charles, George and Mary back to the United Kingdom for their training as doctors. Charles took his degree at Edinburgh and had a practice at Norwich. Later he went to America and settled in California, where he became a successful author, publishing several books, in particular *The Taming of the Jungle* and several volumes of poems. [The book is set in the Kaladhungi of the 1860s.]

George took his degree at Aberdeen, and then practised at Heathfield, in Sussex. Owing to ill health, he was forced to give up this practice, and having been advised that sea air would be beneficial, he became a ship's doctor and sailed around the world three times, eventually returning to India where he practised as a doctor till he died.

Eugene Mary, named after the Empress, for whom Charles Doyle had great admiration, did her training to become a doctor partly in England and then in India. She worked for many years at St Catherine's Hospital in Amritsar. She was greatly beloved by the Indian population, as she used to travel round the villages giving medical aid, and could speak many dialects.[7]

When C.W. Corbett was the postmaster at Naini Tal a stray letter from him in the Municipal Board records of Naini Tal, dated 16 September 1875, says he was ready to meet a Mr Johnson the next day to discuss the disputed boundary of Helen Villa and Wilding Lodge. It is odd for an apothecary to end up as a postmaster—he retired as one—but the times were rather easy for jobs and White men. From 1872 onwards, C.W. Corbett was also a Naini Tal city father. With his background as an apothecary his contribution to the health debates of the Municipal Board must have been valuable.

[7] Ruby Beyts' notes.

On an Easter Sunday, as he was dressing to go to church, he became unwell and had to lie in bed. He died after a few weeks. According to the burial register of St John's Church, Naini Tal, Christopher Corbett, aged fifty-eight, pensioner, died on 21 April 1881. The cause of the death was fatty degeneration of the heart. He was buried next day. The burial ceremony was conducted by the chaplain of Naini Tal, the Rev. F. Olton. St John-in-the-Wildnerness stands on a knoll overlooking the Malli Tal end of the lake. The retirement age was then fifty-five and C.W. Corbett had just had three years to relax in after that.

Christopher William was not the first Corbett to reach Kumaon. The Gurkhas were driven out of Kumaon in 1815 and there was a Maj. Corbett in Almora in the 1840s who was the commandant of the local garrison at Hawalbagh, near Almora. This gentleman, who had a garden there, sold it to the government in 1841 for the planting of tea. John Company reached Kumaon in 1814, when it started a factory at Kashipur to collect the hemp fibre grown in the hills. Kashipur is not quite Kumaon though, for it is far out in the plains.

Of the two settlements, Mussoorie is older than Naini Tal. The first house went up in Mussoorie in 1826. Naini Tal was yet to be 'discovered' by Mr Barron of Rosa in 1841. Jim Corbett however claimed that the town was discovered in 1839 by an enterprising English administrator who put a heavy stone on the head of an unwilling local guide and made him walk for days till he agreed to show the explorer the secret holy lake. The first house that went up in Naini Tal was that of Mr Lushington, fourth Commissioner of Kumaon. St John-in-the-Wilderness was opened in 1848. The motor car reached Naini Tal in 1915, and electricity in 1922.

Jim Corbett's mother, Mary Jane, took a dwelling site in Naini Tal on the Ayarpata Hill 'about the year 1870' with a land tax of Rs 2 an acre. Ayarpata literally means an 'area paved with ayar' (*Andromeda ovalifolia*), a tree which grows with the oak and rhododendron at elevations above 6,000 feet. Over the land, 1.7 acres in extent, she built Gurney House in the 1880s after her husband's death. When the Corbetts moved to Naini Tal, they built a double-storeyed house first and then a cottage on the opposite Cheena hill. The first house was sold in panic for a pittance after the devastating landslide of 1880 and the cottage was dismantled. Gurney House was built with the material of this cottage carried to the other hill. It was feared that more landslides would follow in the area. Mary Jane also owned another house near by, called Clifton.

What does Gurney mean? Webster's *Third New International Dictionary* takes me to a wheeled cot or a stretcher—a house built with the carted building material of a dismantled house? Or was it named after the Quaker, Joseph J. Gurney, who died in 1847?

Gurney House is a veritable Corbett museum, a repository of all his minor trophies, his furniture, books and his mother's piano. The four-bedroomed house has more Corbett possessions than the regular Forest Department museum at Kaladhungi. The attic is full of deer horns, worth a fortune for a Chinese apothecary. Quite a lot of stuff, including Corbett's fishing boat, is stored in two godowns below the dining room.

His furniture is still in use. His old-fashioned writing bureau, where he wrote his first classic, still stands in his study. Over a cupboard stands an elephant tusk, and kept away in a drawer are two tiger skulls marked BMWL. Two empty cannon shells, of World War II vintage perhaps, now used as flower vases, rest over the piano. The drawing room has an African drum he brought home from Tanzania. Among the souvenirs safely tucked away is a charcoal drawing of a boat on a lake. It is signed J. Corbett.

Corbett fans visit Gurney House in droves every summer when the hill station is full. Under a will drafted by the mother on 3 March 1899, half the Gurney House estate was willed to Maggie and half to Archibald, the last born. Archibald died when he was twenty. The estate passed on to Maggie on the mother's death on 16 May 1924. Mary Jane lies buried next to Christopher William, her husband. The cemetery at St John's was especially opened for her by the Archdeacon of Naini Tal 'for having been known and loved for so long in Naini Tal, she had a right to be buried in the cemetery'.[8] The cemetery was crowded by the landslide deaths.

'Mary Jane Corbett of the North-Western Province of British India' also willed that her house, Clifton, should be sold after her death by the executors of her will and the proceeds 'applied in accordance of the will of my deceased husband, first to the payment of 3,000 rupees to each of my sons, Edward James and Archibald D'Arcy, and my daughter, Margaret Winifred, the residue thereof being divided in three shares equally among my sons, Christopher Edward, John Quinton, and Edward James or their heirs.' The Kaladhungi house, known as Arundel, was bequeathed to John Quinton and the piano to Maggie.

Gurney House is just off a stand of giant oaks. It is on the road to Sherwood College if you start from the Malli Tal lake-end. A short, steep slope and a sharp turn lead to the front of the house. The side entrance has a deodar tree with a rambler rose vine trained on it. There are fruit trees— apricots and plums—in the terraced garden run to seed. Like most Naini Tal houses, it has a honeysuckle creeper trained under the eaves. When I visited it of an April the arum lilies and the roses were blooming. Thrushes and tits flitted in the trees. The rear hedge is partly ringal (hill bamboo). A wide verandah on two sides looks towards the hills. The house has big airy rooms, with Mary Jane's piano in the sitting room where it always was. There are two outhouses. Gurney House was not ready for occupation when Corbett was a child. The family then lived opposite the Old Treasury in Malli Tal.

---

[8] Ruby Beyts' notes.

3 Childhood

JIM CORBETT was baptized on 18 October 1875 at St John's Church, Naini Tal, the last but one of the nine children of Christopher William and Mary Jane. Christopher William had the unenviable lot of raising fifteen children on a pittance of a postmaster's salary. These were the three Doyle children, three from his first marriage and nine from the second. But he was fortunate in having Mary Jane as his wife, for by careful management she saw the family through with the active assistance of her daughter by her first marriage, Eugene Mary Doyle.

Naini Tal was a small settlement in the 1870s with houses dotting the hillside and a bazaar at each end of the lake. The boys in the family took a hand in stocking the lean family larder from game available in the forest around Naini Tal, with an occasional hill sambar, kakar (barking deer), gural (Himalayan chamois), kalij pheasant or peura (hill partridge). Tom, who took over the responsibilities of the family as the eldest son after the father's death, was an excellent shot. As a boy Jim too took to larder hunting by taking pot shots at sitting birds.

These were rather hard days for the Corbetts, with half the house rented out. Even the ammunition for Jim's muzzle-loader was in short supply, and every shot fired had to be accounted for with a kill. In winter, when the family moved down to Kaladhungi, the boys replenished the larder with peafowl (it was not protected as the national bird then), jungle-fowl, chital (spotted deer), hog deer, pig and sambar.

The photograph of a watercolour painting of Arundel, the

house at Kaladhungi, which appears in *Jungle Lore* and which was perhaps done by Jim himself according to a family consensus, is largely imaginative. (The original painting is with Douglas Corbett, son of his brother Christopher Edward.) The lifeline of the Kaladhungi area is the Baur river canal built by Sir Henry Ramsay. The Commissioner in those days combined the functions of judge, magistrate, police chief and engineer. The northern boundary of the Arundel estate touches the canal. The ruined house, which is on a slope, faces south. This estate is circumscribed on the east and west by two dry watercourses which meet at its base. Behind the house is dense jungle, and where the watercourses meet there is scrub forest.

An aqueduct carries the Baur canal over the western watercourse to the Kaladhungi bazaar and beyond. This is Bijli Dat (lightning arch), so named because the duct was wrecked by lightning and had to be remade. By the side of the house— an Irish cottage with a big living room—there is a grove of mangoes, and the park-like open space opposite is dotted with semal (silk cotton) and haldu (*Adina cordifolia*) trees. Two Persian lilac trees and lantana bushes now occupy what were the two rear bedrooms of the house.

There could be no place better suited for the making of a naturalist than Arundel. Tigers came to the canal to drink, so did deer. The sandy beds of the two watercourses recorded all wildlife movements by day and night. While studying the sandbeds, young Jim Corbett had his first lessons in the reading of spoor. In the nights he kept track of animals on the move by listening to jungle noises. Kaladhungi, with its location at the foot of the hills, has a fantastic bird life as well. Its jungles receive all the migrants going up to summer in the Himalaya and coming down to winter in the plains. The shady one-mile walk to the head of the Baur canal is lined with silk cotton, runi (*Mallotus philippensis*), khair (*Acacia catechu*) and haldu trees. And above the head of the canal were deep pools in the river teeming with mahseer.

April is the month for birds in Kaladhungi. Migrants

bound for the hills are there as well as residents. On a single April morning, I heard the migrant Indian cuckoo (*Cuculus micropterus*) and the golden oriole in a charivari of birdsong with doves cooing, peafowl meowing and the crow pheasant booming. Drongos were everywhere, and so were bulbuls pouring out their liquid song. I could hear the hoopoe on the telegraph wire and the coppersmith and the green barbet in the ficus trees. Jungle-fowl, peafowl and drongos heralded the dawn. In the mango groves the koel cooed and hordes of noisy parakeets were being driven away by watchmen wielding sling shots.

For Jim's childhood days one has to lean rather heavily on the biographical details scattered throughout his six available books. Alas, the picture that emerges is uneven. Many aspects are not fully covered and many withheld. For instance, the only information he vouchsafes on his father is that he was four when his father died. About his mother he only says that, though she had 'the courage of Joan of Arc and Nurse Cavell combined' she was as 'gentle and as timid as a dove'.[1]

The first Corbett memory is of romps to the edge of the forest at Kaladhungi as an eight-year-old with brother Archie, four, and their Collie, Robin (not to be confused with the Robin buried in the grounds of the 'museum house' and hero of a chapter in *Man-Eaters of Kumaon*). One of the romps nearly ended in disaster for the two boys with an infuriated she-bear attacking them. But the Collie saved their lives. The second Robin was named after him. 'Archie was his constant companion. The two boys were devoted to each other and there was deep understanding between them. They enjoyed doing things together and had the same love of sport and of all that is beautiful in nature. Archie's admiration for Jim, four years his senior, was unbounded, and I do not think there was ever a cross word spoken between the two boys, so great was their affection for each other.'[2]

[1] *Jungle Lore*, p. 14.
[2] Ruby Beyts' notes.

The second memory is of a severe attack of pneumonia and diligent nursing by brother Tom and the sisters Mary Doyle and Maggie. During convalescence, when the daily drinking of beef juice had became hateful, brother Tom presented Jim with his first catapult as an incentive for recovery. With it came the first lessons when not to use it. He was told that for a sportsman there are two seasons, one closed when birds and animals breed or look after the young, and the other when they are not doing so. The catapult had to be put away for the first part, as a bird killed meant an abandoned nest or fledgelings starved to death. Also, he was told, every bird killed had to be made use of—if edible, eaten, otherwise skinned and set for collection. Pigeons and doves went into the pot and others to the collection.

Brother Tom also provided Jim with a skinning knife and arsenical soap and gave him the first lesson in skinning, showing how to dress a kalij pheasant. In the closed season the catapult was used only in competitions the boys held in shooting off the giant semal flowers and hitting other fixed targets. Jim also took long walks with the older boys in the forest on moonlit nights, collected butterflies and raided birds' nests for eggs.

Of the fourteen children of the two White families in Kaladhungi, ranging in age from eight to eighteen—Archie was too young to venture far out of doors—Jim at eight, as the youngest afoot, was saddled with the onerous duty of escorting all seven girls to the canal where they went to bathe on weekdays. It was thought proper that the girls should have an escort young enough not to offend the proprieties. He carried the towels and nighties to the water—there were no swimsuits then—and stood guard on the bank to warn the girls against intruders. For the canal bank was also a thoroughfare for people collecting wood in the forest or working on the canal. If anybody turned up he had to warn the bathers. And if the nighties billowed—they often did as the girls squatted in the canal—he was asked to look the other way.

Every time the boy went out, he was told to keep the girls from harm's way by not allowing them to venture into the deeper waters of the canal. The boy resented this chore for, as the girls bathed, the other boys of the two families had a whale of a time, catapult and rod in hand, running to the headworks of the canal with improvised fishing tackle to catch fish on bent-pin hooks baited with dough. After the fishing, for which there was fierce competition, the boys undressed and jumped into the big pool near the head of the canal and competed again to reach the other bank first.

Corbett recounts his canal-bank assignment with considerable amusement, but this biographer shudders to think what the sights and sounds in the canal did to the child's psyche—the clinging nighties, dark groins and the banal talk revolving round the two boys, Neil and Dansay, both frequent guests of the two families and 'madly in love with all the girls'.[3] It would perhaps be worthwhile for a depth psychologist to go into a possible childhood trauma which kept Corbett away from women and matrimony and made him a kind of ascetic.

On Sundays, which were unaccountably not bathing days for the girls, he was with the boys fishing and splashing in the river. In the evenings, all the boys and girls collected at the Baur bridge (that was the old wooden cantilever which existed before the iron one was erected in 1899); they built a bonfire with the wood collected from the scrub forest and heard ghost stories from Dansay in an Irish setting, with the local banshees and churails thrown in.

In Kaladhungi, unlike Naini Tal, the boys were not quite insulated against the natives. On the canal bank, and in the forest, the sahib boys and village boys mixed freely and played. One patriarch of Kaladhungi remembered well a common Corbett prank of throwing cowdung at a boy as he emerged out of the canal after bathing and waited for sun and wind to towel his skin. As a child, Jim picked up

---

[3] *Jungle Lore*, p. 8.

the local dialect, and in later years, as he continued to mix with the 'natives', he acquired a fair proficiency in all the local dialects of the hills. However, things were quite different in summer. The boys mixed only with the Whites. Naini Tal then was quite colour conscious. The Upper Mall, connecting Talli Tal and Malli Tal (the two lake-ends) was almost entirely the White man's preserve, with only a handful of privileged Indians allowed to share it. The vast majority of Indians, all the porters and laden animals were not allowed to use it till 1932. They had to take the lower road, which was rendered slightly hazardous by those enjoying themselves on horseback.

In his catapult days there came an assignment from Jim's cousin, Stephen Dease—he ended up as a priest—for specimens to illustrate his book on the birds of Kumaon. This made Jim an early ornithologist. Most of the 480 hand-painted illustrations in the book were based on the birds Jim collected for Dease and cured carefully on a string stretched across his bedroom. As he ventured further afield collecting birds, the boy's serious education in jungle sights and sounds began. Sambar and chital, he learnt, ponk or pook when they see a tiger or leopard on the prowl. Kakar bark for the same reason, and they also sometimes do so at humans, snakes and pine martens. Pheasants cackle when carnivore are near. Babblers raise Cain for the same reason and the drongo—a fair mimic of many bird calls and a good one of the chital's warning call—stands as sentry over feeding jungle-fowl and babblers. Also, he noticed that langur and monkeys, deer and jungle-fowl run their own watch-and-ward system against the tiger and leopard.

The application of this knowledge of how the jungle telegraph works, which he unconsciously imbibed from childhood years through adult life, helped Jim become a master sleuth of the wilds, a great sportsman and pioneering wildlife photographer. An early encounter with a porcupine, chased by Dansay's dog Scottie and Tom's Magog—Tom was a veteran of the Second Afghan War—was an eye-opener for the child on how destructive a porcupine quill can be. A quill nearly killed Magog.

In Corbett's later years, when he killed his maneating leopards and tigers and sat for a post-mortem—he had always to satisfy himself about why the animal had taken to killing humanity—he found that quite a lot of them had become so because of broken porcupine quills in festering wounds. It remained an enigma to him all his life why an intelligent animal like the tiger was so clumsy in killing porcupines for food. Leopards are tidier.

Dansay, a general's disinherited son—a Gen. Dansay was living at Lohaghat in eastern Kumaon—who was resting in Kaladhungi after losing a job in the Forest Service and waiting for one in the Political Service, met Jim one day while the boy was demonstrating to his friends how to swing from one branch of a tree to another. Dansay gallantly offered to take him to the Dhunigar forest to show him how a tiger was shot on foot. Though there were a lot of pugmarks they did not see a tiger. While returning home, Dansay, who was carrying two muzzle-loaders, a shotgun and a rifle, decided that it was not too early for the boy to handle his first firearm. A number of white-capped laughing thrushes were feeding on the ground. Unslinging the shotgun, he pointed to the birds and, after telling Jim to put his left foot aside, asked him to fire. This ended in near-calamity. As the muzzle-loader went off with a vicious kick, Jim lay sprawled on the ground. The gun had been flung aside and Dansay was now running his fingers tenderly over the barrel looking for dents. There was no sign of the birds Jim had aimed at. Instead, there was a little thing on the ground, a white-browed flycatcher. This one had died of plain shock. Either Dansay, a thickset man, was in the habit of overcharging his gun or he had sought revenge against Jim, who had conspired with the girls in the canal some time earlier to play a prank on him.

Soon came the great day when brother Tom, to the consternation of their mother, offered to take Jim on a bear shoot.

The brothers went up a big mountain in the oak forest. Skirting a ravine, Jim was left on a rock with a shotgun and two ball cartridges with the parting advice: shoot to kill and not to wound. Tom took up a position on the skyline. That was Jim's first day of terror, when he was left alone in the forest. A dry oak branch, broken by bears feeding on acorns, came crashing down and the boy, who had set out to tell Tom that he had spotted a bear, returned to the rock in a cold sweat. When the sun went down Tom rejoined Jim and they headed for home.

Back in Kaladhungi, Tom took Jim to the Garappu forest to shoot peafowl one December morning. Tom was a great one for an early start and the two left on the seven-mile walk at 4 a.m. with a breakfast of tea and homemade biscuits. At first light they got up from the big well, a famous Garappu landmark, and headed for a patch of ber (*Zizyphus jujuba*). This wayside well, now far out in the river bed, will soon be obliterated if nothing is done to save it. A peafowl flew into a semal tree. Handing over his shotgun, Tom asked Jim to walk ahead. As the boy stalked the bird and stood still to cock his gun, a low whistle summoned him to his mentor, who pointed out that the bird was out of range. Jim explained that he had only stopped to cock the gun. When he went again for the bird, it flew away. Tom, however, collected three peafowl and one jungle-fowl.

With these three lessons Jim's hunting education ended so far as his elders were concerned. He had fired a gun and also known terror. When the rubber of the catapult decayed, he graduated to the pellet bow he got made for himself after seeing the Gurkha guardsmen using it at the Old Treasury opposite their first summer house at Malli Tal. This bow has two strings with a bit of webbing in the centre to hold a stone. After drawing the webbing with the nesting stone, the left hand, which holds the bow, has to be deftly twisted to avoid injury. He gained such proficiency in using this bow that he could defeat the top Gurkha marksman in hitting a matchbox placed on a post twenty yards away.

Then followed a bow-and-arrow Red Indian period after reading Fenimore Cooper. The Kumaon hills have no tradition of bowmanship, and in the absence of a pattern the end product was unsatisfactory. The arrows were tipped with nails. But then came another great day when Stephen Dease presented Jim with a gun in return for the specimens supplied for his bird book. In between, a childhood fantasy of becoming a lumberman in Canada had led Jim to learn how to split a matchstick in two with an axe.

Dease's gun, an old warrior, had a split right barrel, and the stock and barrels were held together with brass wire. Jim was eight now. As the news spread that the boy had got his first gun, 'Uncle' Kunwar Singh, his 'poacher friend' and head of Chandni Chowk village, near Kaladhungi, came to congratulate him and welcome him into the fraternity of local hunters. When the gun was handed to him for inspection, the visitor discreetly ignored the condition of the right barrel and only extolled the virtues of the left, commenting on the good service it was capable of. With it came the advice: 'You are no longer a boy but a man; and with this good gun you can go anywhere you like in our jungle and never be afraid provided you learn how to climb trees'.[4]

Later, after Jim had bagged his first leopard, came acceptance and an invitation from Kunwar Singh for a shoot in the Garappu forest. There the boy presented himself one dawn in his first pair of shorts, much to the disapproval of 'uncle'. Corbett stuck to shorts all his life. For years 'uncle' and 'nephew' shot together, the 'uncle' imparting all the knowledge he had of the Kaladhungi forest. From him Jim learnt how to make mental maps to retrieve game left in the forest, reckon distances by the flight of muzzle-loader bullets, how not to be afraid of forest fires, and lastly how to climb trees fast in an emergency. Rubber-soled canvas shoes had not been invented and the boy discarded his leather shoes to be more agile in climbing trees.

[4] *My India*, p. 19.

With the one intact barrel of his gun the boy kept the family larder well stocked for two winters in Kaladhungi and even managed to kill a chital with No. 4 shot. The gun gave him confidence to range far and wide, and on one occasion to track down Dansay's alleged banshee during a storm in the forest. He found that the banshee sigh was coming from the branches of two trees rubbed together by the wind. The investigation of the churail however came later, after World War I (the 'Kaiser's war' for Jim), when he heard it on the haldu tree fifty yards away from the 'museum house', where he lived at that time. A bird called some twenty times, its beak pointing upwards. He describes its call as that of 'a soul in torment'. With all his ornithological background, Corbett could not identify it. The call was 'something apart, something that does not appear to have any connexion with our world and that has the effect of curdling the hearer's blood and arresting his heartbeats'.[5] The tree is no longer there.

Though better armed with the muzzle-loader, Jim was still afraid of the tiger. Shooting nearer home, he never ventured into the forest if he found tiger tracks leading only one way. His first encounter with a tiger was in Naya Gaon, three miles from Kaladhungi, while hunting birds with Magog. Seven peafowl led the dog after crossing a glade to a sleeping tiger. The dog yelped, the peafowl squawked, and in the bedlam the tiger chased the dog, uttering roar after roar. Unashamedly, the master deserted the dog and ran for his life. Magog soon joined him. The tiger gave up the chase and stopped roaring.

Soon after, avoiding the denser forest because of tigers, Jim stepped on a coiled python in a depression while inching his way to get a shot at a jungle-fowl. He fired into the depression and ran for his life again. Back at Naini Tal, dog and master had their first encounter with a leopard disturbed by milkmen returning home from the town to their village below Sarya Tal. The leopard merely took a close look at the

[5] *Jungle Lore*, p. 4.

two and bounded away. Corbett liked to think both the tiger and the leopard somehow could sense the harmless nature of the encounter. In the first place the roars were just to shoo off an intruder, and in the second a close look was enough to dismiss a small boy and his dog looking for pheasant.

Maggie recollects that after their father died

Mother was left with a number of young children to bring up and educate, a big responsibility, and had she not been as full of courage as she was, it would have been very hard for her. She seems to have shouldered her burden bravely. I have often thought that Jim inherited many of her characteristics: bravery, courage, generosity and kindliness combined with a high sense of duty. Although she never punished us, she expected implicit obedience from us, and I do not think she was disappointed. In appearance she was very small, with delicate features, lovely colouring and beautiful blue eyes. She was just the sort of mother to bring up boys. She did not fuss with them, and allowed them to follow their own natural bent in things that interested them. She was utterly unselfish and never felt that any self-denial or self-sacrifice on her part was too great where her children were concerned, and how many things she must have had to do without.

Our half sister, Mary, was a great help to Mother in the education and general care of the younger children. A room in the house was set aside as a schoolroom, in which a school routine was observed with regular hours and a strict discipline. This was continued until we were old enough to go to school and to take our place with other children. Mary was musical and taught us to sing duets, and at times we would be called upon to perform before our elders. This we did, not at all enjoying the publicity, but we would not have thought of disobeying an elder sister. Jim had a very clear treble voice which later developed into a beautiful tenor.

We also learned to play a number of instruments, Jim on the guitar, the banjo, and the flute, whilst I played the piano. We had a Shirdmayer piano, a most beautiful instrument with a lovely tone. When we reached teenage, Mother would sometimes let us have a carpet dance in the big drawing room at Gurney House, and we would have great fun with our young friends. The girls took turns at playing the piano. We could dance most of the popular dances of the day: the mazurka, Schottische, polka, and the square dances such as the Lancers, Roger de Coverley, quadrilles, etc.

Those were such happy days, and in fact we had a wonderfully happy childhood, although the strictest economy had to be observed and we did without many things which in this more luxurious age would be deemed necessities.

The lake in Naini Tal afforded us the greatest pleasure, as with a ringal rod, thread and bent pin, we extracted many small fish from its deep waters. Jim soon began to catch bigger fish, and was once stopped by the Deputy Commissioner, who told him jokingly that he would have to take out a licence if he were going to catch such big fish. All through his life Jim loved fishing on the Naini lake, and often said he would rather fish there than anywhere else even after he had fished in many parts of the world. He used the lightest tackle and would stand for hours in a boat, fly-fishing. Some days we would start from home early enough to be at the further end of the lake by dawn, when Jim would begin fishing and continue until we caught sight of our man coming down the hill with a basket containing the early morning chota hazri consisting of tea and toast which Mary had prepared for us. The boat would then be drawn up to a quiet spot on the bank where we would enjoy the very welcome meal.[6]

We don't know in what year Jim shifted to Oak Openings School on the Sher-ka-Danda hill. After four ups and downs it now functions as Birla Vidya Mandir. Earlier, it was Philander Smith College and Hallett War School. Incidentally, it is one of the highest schools in India at an altitude of 7,500 feet. Here in 1876, the last mountain quail (*Ophrysia superciliosa*) was shot and thus became extinct.

Jim's first school was a private one of some seventy boys lorded over by a tyrant of an ex-serviceman known for his dexterity with the cane. This earned him the title 'Dead-Eye Dick' from the boys. The school was probably Petersfield. At ten, Jim became the youngest cadet of the Voluntary Rifles. This unit was formed in 1871, became the 10th Naini Tal Company in 1917, and Naini Tal Rifles in 1920. It later grew into the Auxiliary Force, raised from Whites and Anglo-Indians to provide a second line of defence in troubled times.

The cadet company paraded at the Flats and had target

[6] Ruby Beyts' notes.

practice at the Sukha Tal firing range where, as the youngest cadet, Jim was once selected to show his marksmanship to a visiting officer. This officer later became Field-Marshal Earl Roberts. In the excitement the boy forgot to fix the sights of the ·450 Martini rifle and the first round went haywire to the consternation of the onlookers. The kindly officer set the sight right, and the cadet then acquitted himself well. This was the first time he came in contact with a celebrity-to-be, and in later years Corbett wrote about the encounter: 'When I have been tempted, as many times I have been, to hurry over a shot or over a decision, the memory of that quiet voice telling me to take my time has restrained me and I have never ceased to be grateful to the great soldier who gave me that advice.'[7]

The performance, which cost Jim a sore shoulder, for this rifle has a vicious kick, pleased the Sergeant-Major. It earned Jim the private use of a similar rifle from the armoury of the Cadet Corps when the winter vacation started. The Sergeant-Major lent it to him for the vacation provided he kept it clean. The boy was thrilled. This was his first rifle, and the ammunition was free.

Back at Kaladhungi, Jim abandoned the muzzle-loader and shot even game birds with the rifle. This form of shooting can be wasteful, for the meat may be spoiled. So he learnt exactly where to shoot, taking mostly head shots. Armed with the powerful rifle, the boy ventured where he had never been before. One of these areas was the Farm Yard, called so at home because it was 'crawling' with jungle-fowl and tigers. The Kota-Kaladhungi road, which runs north a little beyond the bridge on the Baur, passes through the Farm Yard, which is bounded by the right bank of the Baur river.

His intention now, as a boy's would be to show off, was to kill a pig for the village with his newly acquired firearm. This was a habit which he kept up most of his sporting life. Old villagers ruefully remember that it was always tough meat they got, for in later years he picked the oldest animal in the

[7] *Jungle Lore*, p. 85.

herd for sacrifice. One day, as he trained his rifle at a jungle-fowl, a leopard bounded towards Jim. He fired at the leopard, and to his consternation the animal jumped right over and landed behind him. There was blood on the rock where he was standing and all over his clothes. The cautious stalking for the wounded animal began, and as it turned its head to look at the hunter a careful shot through the ear stilled it.

So great was his excitement at bagging his first leopard that Corbett decided to tie the carcass with a creeper and carry it home. But he could not do so because it was too heavy. He was not aware then that it was risky to shoot a tiger or leopard facing one at a higher elevation, and the outcome could have been serious for him if the leopard had landed on him. The boy 'trembled with joy at the beautiful animal' he had shot and in 'anticipation of the pleasure'[8] of carrying the news home.

He ran three miles for help to carry his trophy home. And who else would accompany him and the two household servants to the Farm Yard but sister Maggie? She doted on her younger brother and kept close to him all her life, and even after death to rest in a common grave. In later years she became his housekeeper, confidante and mother-figure all in one, ministering to his needs, herself satisfied only with the reflected glory of the hunter.

Earlier we noted the straitened circumstances of the Corbetts. The existence of two servants can well be explained as the attempt of a White family to keep the flag flying with some pretence at opulence. It always had to be on guard against the danger of going 'native'.

The first tiger was shot much later. This was 'accomplished on foot with an old army rifle which I bought for fifty rupees from a seafaring man, who I am inclined to think had stolen it and converted it into a sporting rifle'.[9]

Now, with his newly acquired confidence and the rifle, Jim

[8] *Jungle Lore*, p. 90.
[9] *The Temple Tiger*, p. 185.

took to camping in the wilds. The first basic lessons in jungle craft, to interpret and mimic bird and animal calls and read signs on the game track, had been acquired. Whatever fear of the forest he had went 'by sleeping anywhere he happened to be when night came on, with a small fire to give him company and warmth, wakened at intervals by the callings of tigers, sometimes in the distance, at other times near at hand; throwing another stick on the fire and turning over and continuing his interrupted sleep without one thought of unease; knowing from his short experience and from what others, who like himself have spent their days in the jungles, had told him, that a tiger, unless molested, would do him no harm. . . .'[10]

Apparently these exploits were not undertaken alone. According to Maggie, 'from the age of about nine or ten, Jim used to go off into the jungle for several days and nights at a stretch, accompanied by our gardener, an old and trusted family servant, as indeed all Indian servants were. They would light a fire at night to keep the tigers away, and during the day would observe wildlife and learn the way of the jungle. It was at this time that Jim began to imitate the calls of wild animals and birds. Although he never came to any harm, I can't help feeling Mother must have had some anxious moments, although she never showed any disquietude.'[11]

Apart from courage, which he got as his confidence grew, Corbett was blessed with an excellent memory, good sight, a sound constitution, and a keen power of observation and hearing. Because he was raised in the hills he was 'as sure-footed as a goat'.[12] As for endurance, carrying a wet tiger skin weighing forty pounds for fifteen miles on a hill track was nothing to him even at the age of fifty-five.

How did the boy fare at his studies? Apart from the activities of the Cadet Corps and the prowess of the principal of

[10] *Man-Eaters of Kumaon*, p. 13.
[11] Ruby Beyts' notes.
[12] *The Temple Tiger*, p. 150.

Petersfield with the cane, Corbett has written very little about his schools. 'Jim was removed from this school and sent to another larger establishment run by the American Methodist Mission where he was very happy and soon became a favourite with masters and boys alike. He was never very fond of lessons nor the routine of school life, but he loved reading and Fenimore Cooper was one of his favourite authors. At night in the dormitory he would read *The Pathfinder* or some other exciting book aloud to the other boys clustered around his bed.'[13]

If the canal-bank childhood trauma took Corbett to the asceticism of a White sadhu, it was Fenimore Cooper, the novelist of the early settler period in North America, who made him choose a romantic way of life markedly Cooperian. We find him all the time unconsciously playing the role of the Cooper hero Natty Bumppo of the Leatherstocking Tales, retreating into the wilds and continuing his relentless fight against advancing civilization, upholding the principles he stood for—courage, love of justice, truth, reverence and integrity. Bumppo is Hawkeye in *The Last of the Mohicans*.

His style of writing too follows Cooper's. 'The happy hunting grounds', the American Indian concept of heaven, is a Cooper expression he used in closing the story of Robin in *Man-Eaters of Kumaon*.

In his brief but prolific literary career (1820–51), Cooper, novelist, social critic and historian, wrote thirty-three novels and sundry non-fiction. The setting of most of his novels was the prairies, where the American Indian was being relentlessly pushed out by White settlers. *The Pathfinder* (1840) was part of the Leatherstocking series beginning with *The Pioneers* and ending with *The Deerslayer*, which deals with the westward march of White civilization and the wanton exploitation of nature's bounty by the 'Palefaces'.

Leatherstocking, lover of the wilderness, philosopher, hunter and scout, opens the way for the settlers and himself

[13] Ruby Beyts' notes.

ruins the wilderness, aware of the wrong being done to nature. To him the wilderness was the creation of God in which man could learn humility and restraint. Cooper too was the eleventh child of the twelve his parents had.

I doubt whether Jim did his Senior Cambridge. If he had, as a Domiciled Englishman he would have qualified for a better government job. Also, seeing how proud he was in later years of his army rank, I should like to think he would have preferred the Indian Army as a career. But the commissioned ranks of the army were virtually barred to Anglo-Indians and Domiciled Englishmen—sneeringly called 'country bottled'—before the turn of the century in the prevailing tight caste system. Only in war were the portals of officerdom open to them. Corbett rushed three times to arms as the opportunity came. Besides, he volunteered for the Boer War, but was not released by the railways.

According to *Current Biography* (1946 edition), Corbett wanted to go in for engineering after school, but the family finances did not permit that. The three government departments then open to an impecunious Irish lad were the Post and Telegraph, the Railways and the Customs, where poor Whites enjoyed quota reservations with the Anglo-Indians. His father had served in the postal department and brother Tom was there, so the boy decided to branch out towards the railways, with his childhood fantasies of driving locomotives perhaps acting subconsciously as a motivating force. He appeared at an interview for a job, but was rejected because of his age. Corbett, according to Cumberlege, told his interviewer: 'You tell me I am too young to begin work, but if I came next year you would tell me I was too old.'[14]

So Corbett went from school, a stripling of eighteen, straight to Bihar to work as a temporary fuel inspector of the Bengal and North-Western Railway on a salary of Rs 100 a month. BNWR's locomotives still ran on wood fuel and coal

[14] Introduction to *Man-Eaters of Kumaon* and *The Temple Tiger*, World's Classics edition.

engines, though ready, had not yet been put on the metre-gauge track. This entailed considerable destruction of forests in the making of billets that went into locomotives' furnaces. He had to look after a large labour force, organize felling, billeting, stowing and carting fuel and disbursing wages.

4 Railway Days

IT IS odd that a naturalist should start his career with the destruction of the forest and its wildlife which he so loved. But this was perhaps a necessary phase for Corbett to become aware of the problem. The youthful railway fuel inspector pitched his tent on the left bank of the Ganga ten miles from the metre-gauge track to organize the felling. The boy was used to a hard life. The itch to hunt was there, but the work was so strenuous by day that he had to take to night fishing and hunting to stock his larder.

This was done by the waxing moon, for he soon discovered that if the moon was not caught on the gunsight the shot went wide. Unashamedly, he confesses he shot roosting peafowl and stalked chital, pig and four-horned antelope by night. The first lessons in forest ecology were also learnt with the creation of a menagerie of the waifs he found in the felled forest. These were Rex the python, partridge and peafowl chicks, leverets and the young of two four-horned antelopes. They were all returned to the forest when they grew up. One of the young antelopes was Tiddley-de-Winks, who refused to leave and nearly got killed in a misadventure because of her confiding nature.

It was a two-year assignment, but the work ended in eighteen months. With the disuse of the wood engine—it took billets only 36 inches long—the fuel inspector became redundant. He was summoned to Samastipur, the regional headquarters of the railway, to hand over charge. There he went with his books carefully balanced and to return Rs 200 of unaccounted money which the cartmen in his employ had left with him without leaving a forwarding address.

After the books had been carefully checked by Ryles, head of the locomotive department, the boy slipped out leaving the money in a string bag on the table. He had been warned by an old railway hand not to leave money after balancing accounts. The bag was spotted. The boy was in a panic. He was closely questioned and was asked to face Izat, the Agent (general manager) of the railway, the next day.

Izat was satisfied with Corbett's version of the matter. Corbett was then asked why he had not pocketed the money, since he could have done so without exposure. His answer pleased Izat, and with that he was told that he could have another job with the railway. The unaccounted money went to the welfare fund started for railway widows and orphans.

The new job at Samastipur lasted a year, with miscellaneous duties as guard, assistant storekeeper and assistant station master. Part of the time Corbett rode the footplates of the engines, checking fuel consumption. He liked this job, for it fulfilled a childhood ambition.

General apprenticeship over, Corbett was now asked to report to Storrar, the ferry superintendent at Mokameh Ghat, and then to the railway's headquarters at Gorakhpur, where he was told that he had been appointed trans-shipment inspector at Mokameh Ghat with a raise of Rs 50 a month. After a week he was to take over the contract for handling goods for the BNWR there. So to Mokameh Ghat he went with Rs 150 as savings to do a job about which he hadn't the vaguest idea.

Seeing the congestion at the yards of the metre-gauge line (the railway that summer had closed bookings to Mokameh Ghat), he knew the task was not easy. The White staff were discouraging, but in Ram Saran, the station master, he found an ally. When Ram Saran said 'we will manage', Corbett made up his mind and wired his assent to headquarters. When the local railway employees were confronted with the order, they were stunned. Clearance of goods from one gauge

to another was a chronic problem at the yards and an inex-
perienced boy, not yet twenty-one, was hardly the person to
handle it.

Mokameh Ghat, on the right bank of the Ganga, was a
focal point on the railway system. On the right bank of the
river was the broad-gauge railway and on the left the metre-
gauge. Both systems ran roughly parallel to the river with
branches radiating north and south. Opposite Mokameh Ghat
was Samaria Ghat, the river terminus of the metre-gauge
system. Before the Mokameh bridge was built, the river here
was five miles wide in the monsoon and trans-shipment of
goods was done by a fleet of river steamers. To start with, one
single labour company handled the goods for both systems.
This was found unsatisfactory as the congestion continued,
and in summer particularly, when traffic was at its peak, the
railway had perforce to stop bookings temporarily, which
resulted in a considerable loss of revenue.

Within a week Corbett organized his labour force of twelve
headmen, eleven of whom were to recruit ten men each, and
the twelfth a gang of sixty men and women to clear coal. All
worked sixteen hours a day clearing goods through the week,
Sundays and festival days included. Besides the labour force,
he had to supervise a staff of over 200 clerks, pointsmen,
shunters and watchmen. To start with, some 500,000 tons
of goods had to be cleared. Those were spartan days, as indi-
cated by Corbett in the following lines:

> 'What was on the plate you put in front of the Sahib?'
> 'A chapati and a little dal.'
> 'Why only one chapati and only a little dal?'
> 'Because there is no money to buy more.'
> 'What else does the Sahib eat?'
> 'Nothing.' [1]

The diner was Corbett, the newly appointed contractor handling the goods of the BNWR at Mokameh Ghat. The
questioner in the verandah was one of the headmen of his

[1] *My India*, p. 148.

labour gang leading a deputation of eleven others and the men under them who had not been paid for three months. The man replying to the questions was Corbett's house servant, who had just served dinner.

That was the contractor's first meal after spending three hours of a hot day putting a derailed railway engine back on the track at Samaria Ghat, on the opposite bank of the Ganga, after two efforts with handjacks. The contractor was not particularly cheerful. He had reasons not to be, for he had not been paid for three months either. His own meagre savings of Rs 150 from two and a half years of work had nearly gone.

When the plate was cleared, the headman with the henna-dyed beard entered: 'We came to tell you that our stomachs have long been empty and that after tomorrow it would be no longer possible for us to work. But we have seen tonight that your case is as bad as ours and we will carry on as long as we have strength to stand. I will, with your permission, go now, Sahib, and, for the sake of Allah, I beg you to do something to help us.'

These first three months of the goods handling contract had been a nightmare, with four hours' sleep nightly on a half-empty stomach. Despite weekly reminders the railway headquarters at Gorakhpur had not sent the necessary money. The workmen had pawned their trinkets and now the headmen had come to apprise him of the grim state of affairs. Corbett rushed to the telegraph office and got the line cleared for an urgent telegram to headquarters: 'Work at Mokameh Ghat ceases at midday today unless I am assured that twelve thousand rupees has been dispatched by morning train.'[2] Two days later, the money arrived, and with it the youthful contractor tided over his worst crisis.

When the pay clerk from headquarters arrived with twelve bags of Rs 1,000 each and Corbett's own three months' salary of Rs 450 in brand-new currency notes, the labour force took

[2] *My India*, p. 149.

half a day off. Corbett slept soundly the rest of the day. There were no further troubles in all the twenty-one years he handled the contract. There was not a day's interruption of work, not even when he was away in France during World War II. When he finally left Mokameh Ghat, he was handling a million tons of goods a year.

What was the secret of his success? The rates were the lowest paid to any railway contractor. Corbett puts it down to the absence of trade unionists (grousers mostly) and of slave drivers and the general will of an average person to better his lot. His men made more money than those in the old labour company. Then he distributed eighty per cent of his profits to his workmen as bonus. This came to about a month's extra earnings.

As life became organized, Corbett, at the instance of Ram Saran, opened a school for the children of his workmen and the low-paid railway staff. It started with twenty boys, and when the number of teachers had gone up to seven the government took over and made it a middle school and later a high school. Here caste prejudices intervened, for children of the upper and lower castes would not sit in one hut. But the problem was solved with the removal of the hut's side walls, for a shed was acceptable.

This done, Corbett turned to sports and trained his own football and hockey teams for the inter-railway tournaments. In this he found an ally in Tom Kelly, the station master of the broad-gauge system, who also raised his own football and hockey teams. The matches were well attended. Kelly, because of his bulk, stayed at the goalpost but Corbett, more agile, played as a forward. The respect for the contractor was carried to the playground. Whenever he tripped, to his embarrassment the game was stopped till his clothes had been dusted.

Later, his railway gave its four White staff a club with a tennis court and a billiard table. The tennis court was not in much use but the table was, nightly. Kelly of the other gauge was made an honorary member.

In winter, with a bit of leisure, Kelly's broad-gauge station trolley was put to good use when the migrant barheaded and greylag geese came in. At sundown the two trolleyed down nine miles out to the tanks along the track and shot geese by moonlight as they rose from the islands in the river to feed on the crops. About the hunting, Corbett wrote: 'Those winter evenings, when the full moon was rising over the palm trees that fringed the river, and the cold brittle air throbbed and reverberated with the honking of geese and the swish of their wings as they passed overhead in flights of from ten to a hundred, are among the happiest of my recollections of the years I spent at Mokameh Ghat.'[3]

The year's big day was Christmas, when a bonus was distributed to the staff. Custom ordained that the Sahib should stay at home till 10 a.m. to be escorted to the office by Ram Saran with the flowing beard and red turban. The station's red and green signal flags were fixed as buntings, the best roses were tightly bunched in a metal flower vase on the office table. Sweets were distributed to the children and speeches made. The inaugural act was a jasmine garland slipped over Corbett's head by Ram Saran.

Corbett's house was 200 yards from the river. He shared it for a time with Storrar, till that official left the place on promotion. Part of the time Corbett's mother stayed with him. He had a servant, a waterman and a punkah coolie.

Habitually, he had his bath at 8 p.m. One night he found himself with a cobra in the bathroom of his three-room cottage. It seemed ages as the man and reptile watched each other. In a panic move, the kerosene lantern lighting the bathroom was extinguished, and when Corbett heard his servant laying the table for dinner he called for help. Another lantern was put into the bathroom through a broken windowpane. In the dim light Corbett killed the snake by dropping the wooden bathstand over its neck. A swift step to the door, the bolt undone, he ran into a crowd of excited men wielding sticks. He had soap in his eyes and not a stitch on!

[3] *My India*, p. 177.

The apothecary's son came in handy every mango season when cholera struck. At all hours of the day and night he was there to help the afflicted with his bag of primitive medicine—rubbing ginger powder on the soles and palms was one remedy for warmth—and his unbounded confidence that, if there was a will to live, nothing more was needed. He nursed many victims through in his simple way, but he could not save Chamari, the headman of his labour gang, for all his efforts. However, he saved Lalaji by picking up the dying man from the bank of the river. A grain merchant who had seen better days, Lalaji was friendless and a total stranger. He was put in the punkah coolie's room and nursed to recovery. Having heard his story, Corbett impulsively gave him Rs 500, most of his savings, to rehabilitate him as a businessman. Lalaji dutifully returned the money within a year as promised. Corbett declined the twenty-five per cent interest offered.

Another kind act was freeing a workman (Budhu of *My India*) from the clutches of a usurious moneylender of his village. The moneylender got free labour from Budhu and his wife every harvesting season because Budhu's father had once borrowed Rs 2 from him. This cost Corbett Rs 225.

Even in his railway days Corbett was summoned to kill at least three maneaters. The Champawat maneater was the first. The year 1910 was important to him, for he killed the Mukteswar and Panar maneaters in that year and his workmen at Mokameh Ghat set a record by clearing 5,500 tons of goods in a single day without any mechanical aid. He spent all his annual leave of three weeks at Kaladhungi.

From his earliest days, Jim had a very real sense of responsibility, especially towards the family, and was ever conscious of its financial difficulties. As soon as he went out into the world and began to earn his living, he started to help financially with the education of Archie, even though this meant going without many necessities himself. He had never known anything different and as a boy in school his pocket money was only four annas a week.[4]

[4] Ruby Beyts' notes.

He had been at Mokameh Ghat sixteen years 'when Kaiser Wilhelm started his war'. Corbett rushed to Calcutta to get himself a commission. But the army would not have anything to do with a man of thirty-eight. Rebuffed here, he went to his native Kumaon and by 1917 had raised a labour force for service in France. He accompanied a contingent of 500 men named the 70th Kumaon Labour Corps. The railway at first refused him permission to leave, but when he gave an assurance that the contract continued and work would go on, he was allowed to go.

With the rank of captain, he brought back his entire unit intact except for one man who died of seasickness. He stuck to his men in France, never leaving them even for a day. He even declined a short trip to England because his men would be helpless without him. Like a patriarch, he watched them, kept their money and arranged to pay them on their return in newly-minted silver rupees. Corbett often used to boast that he took 500 men to war and brought back 499.

His second visit to Britain was in 1928, and the subsequent ones in 1951 and 1953. We do not know on what sectors the Corps operated but Corbett, writing about his binoculars (the churail encounter in *Jungle Lore*) says they were used for spotting enemy artillery and planes. On his return, he served in Waziristan in 1919 during the third Anglo-Afghan war. This incidental information we owe to a mention of his buying an Afridi stabbing knife from the government store at Hangu in the North-West Frontier Province (now in Pakistan). It had three notches, the history of a knife responsible for three killings.[5]

Work went on smoothly at Mokameh Ghat in his absence, and he returned to his work force 'with the pleasant feeling that I had been away from them for a day. My safe return was attributed by them to the prayers they had offered up for me in temple and mosque, and at private shrines.'[6]

[5] *The Man-Eating Leopard of Rudraprayag*, p. 127.
[6] *My India*, p. 169.

Perhaps Corbett stayed for a year at Mokameh Ghat after his return from the war. He then handed over the contract to Ram Saran and made for the hills to personally look after a business he had acquired at Naini Tal in 1906. He left with great satisfaction a job well done. There had not been a day's labour trouble and never any unpleasantness, save a man discharged for habitual drunkenness. Looking back at those railway days four years before his death, Corbett wrote to a friend: 'It was a hard life, but I enjoyed every day of it.'[7]

After World War I we find him shooting in Kashmir with Lionel Fortescue, and with Robert Bellairs at the base of Trishul in Kumaon. He had gone to Kashmir to collect a hangal, a cousin of the Scottish red deer, and to the Trishul area for a bharal (wild sheep) and tahr (antelope). The Trishul hunting was abandoned because of a sick porter who had to be taken to Naini Tal for care. Incidentally, medicine could not help Bala Singh, the porter, who languished and died convinced he had swallowed a ghost.[8]

Fortescue, a former housemaster at Eton, and Corbett were in Kashmir with their cameras and fishing rods. Corbett, who had a permit for a Kashmir stag, ventured alone into a 12,000-foot-high range without a guide, to get one. He was caught in a hailstorm. After the storm he saw a hind on a knoll doing sentry duty for the herd. As there was no cover for a closer approach, he sat behind a rock. Corbett now decided to call the herd into the open. First he gave the leopard call. The hind stamped the ground with her forefeet to convey the warning, but that did not draw the herd nearer. So Corbett shifted, exposing his brown tweed coat a little from the cover of the rock. The hind belled. First a yearling joined her, then all six stags and hinds. But it was not enough for him. He wanted to hear the stag call as well. So he shifted again and heard him call. He could have got his stag at 36 yards, but did not.

[7] Letter to J.S. Negi.
[8] *The Temple Tiger*, p. 5.

My pass permitted me to shoot one stag and for all I knew one of the stags might have carried a record head, but though I had set out that morning to look for a stag, and procure meat for the camp, I now realized that I was in no urgent need of a trophy. In any case the stag's meat would probably be tough, so instead of using the rifle, I stood up, and six of the most surprised deer in Kashmir vanished out of sight, and a moment later I heard them crashing through the undergrowth on the far side of the knoll.[9]

Corbett related that, while returning, he took a swipe at an albino musk deer, taking it for a goat. He missed its forefeet and the musk deer continued to sneeze defiance at him after it had regained its composure.

Now this story is rather too thick to swallow, unless the deer was sick or doped. Corbett liked to pull people's legs. P.R. Sherred, who worked in Allen Orchards at Mukteswar in the early 1920s, wrote of an evening spent with the hunter at Jeolikote, when he regaled his audience with the tale of a hamadryad travelling downhill hooplike, with tail in mouth, and talking of the merits of snakes and lizards as food.[10]

Incidentally, Fortescue, who maintained a journal called the Chenab Diary, 1921, does not mention the incident.

[9] *The Man-Eating Leopard of Rudraprayag*, p. 118.
[10] *Corbett Centenary Souvenir*, p. 11.

5 City Father and Businessman

THE YEAR 1906 was a turning point in Corbett's life, with his acquisition of a business at Naini Tal. It was a windfall that made him a man of means. Lord Hailey, his friend, called it an 'inheritance'.[1] The benefactor was Frederick Edward George Matthews, proprietor of F.E.G. Matthews & Company, House and Commission Agents, Hardware Merchants and Auctioneers. Matthews was also for sixteen years a city father of Naini Tal who fought for the right of Indians to use the Upper Mall, barred to them by zealous Anglo-Indian police sergeants. Matthews died childless on 21 September 1906. Mary Matthews, the widow who inherited the business and several houses under her husband's will drawn up on 10 July 1894, sold the business to Corbett on 15 December 1906 'for a consideration of 60,000 rupees'.

That was a lot of money for Corbett in 1906. His railway salary could not have been more than Rs 200 a month and the profits he made from the contract at Mokameh Ghat were not substantial. Eighty per cent of these, as he admits, were shared by his workmen. Even about the later years, he writes of the regular skimping entailed to erect the three-mile-long anti-pig wall round his own estate at the village of Choti Haldwani. This property, opposite Arundel, he bought for Rs 1,500.

This state of affairs is confirmed by a caustic note on Corbett's new village in a revenue report of 4 December 1916. It says: 'Cultivation increasing slightly, probably owing to the

[1] *American Book-of-the-Month Club News*, March 1946.

new pig-fencing [not to be confused with the wall which came up later] put up by Mr Corbett last year at his own expense. It is a pity that he is always in arrears with his payments; he does pay eventually but in the mean time trouble is caused to everyone concerned.'

One could give Corbett the benefit of the doubt over such delays in payment. It was a war year. His sisters, Mary Doyle and Maggie, who looked after his business after 1909 while he was away, were perhaps too preoccupied with the affairs of Matthews & Co., the concern they were running for him. Or was it plain and simple absentee landlordism?

According to legend in Naini Tal, Corbett got the concern free. Matthews, not having an heir, treated him like an adopted son. A sick man for years before his death, he had been neglecting his business, and the concern had been mort-gaged to the Allahabad Bank, Naini Tal, for Rs 60,000.

Most childless people have a continuity complex that often goes into the setting up of marble name slabs to mark their donating money for a good cause. Matthews, who was very attached to the business, wanted it run by somebody after he had gone. The survival of the signboard of F.E.G. Matthews & Co., instead of a marble slab, could perhaps satisfy him. The sale deed of December 1906 clearly says that the concern was passed on to Corbett for a consideration of Rs 60,000. An interesting clause in the deed is that the arrangement was 'according to the wish of the late Mr Frederick Edward George Matthews'. Corbett figures as Mr James Edward Corbett, 'house proprietor', Naini Tal, in the deed.

Corbett might have made his own financial arrangement with the bank, raising on his own some five to ten per cent of the initial money involved and securing another mortgage. There were a lot of good bungalows in the property and the bank could keep the deed as security.

Corbett now acquired the Dudley Grove estate with about four and a half acres of land, Mary Ville with about two acres, Newbery Lodge with about one and a half acres, and Wood-stock and Woodstock Lime Kiln with two acres. The stock in the Matthews hardware shop was priced at Rs 10,000. The goodwill was apparently free.

In August 1906 Corbett had bought a house in Naini Tal, Mullacloe Estate, to qualify for nomination to the municipal board to represent the class of proprietors. Naini Tal had a fully nominated civic board. Matthews died in September that very year, and it would seem as if Corbett was being groomed for his future role of Matthews' choosing as a municipal councillor and new proprietor of the company.

The years 1907 to 1909 are a bit confusing, for we find the railway employee-cum-contractor at Mokameh Ghat being nominated a member of the Naini Tal Municipal Board. What were Corbett's plans? I think he wanted to return for good to Naini Tal to look after the business. Otherwise, why should he have got himself nominated to the Board? There is no mention of his attending Board meetings in 1908 in the annual report. In 1909 he resigned his seat.

Corbett became a member of the Board for three years to fill 'the place vacated by the Rev. F.L. Neel, representing the class of proprietors', with effect from 1 July 1907. On 1 July 1910, J.R. Muirhead took his place. But Corbett managed to attend some meetings in his period of office, perhaps on his holidays, and figures in a report submitted to the Board on the recovery of toll from a resident who brought stone into the town.

In 1911, we find his stepsister Mary Doyle running the business and signing the papers for F.E.G. Matthews & Co. In 1917, a war year, Corbett, finding it difficult to run the business, gave Mary Doyle and Maggie the power of attorney 'to be my true and lawful attorneys, to act for me and in my name and on my behalf and in the name and on behalf of my said firm of F.E.G. Matthews & Co. either jointly or severally'. Did he do this because Maggie felt neglected or Mary Doyle, afflicted with a mental ailment, was showing warning signs?

Corbett and his attorneys did well in business from 1908 to 1934, buying and selling houses owned mostly by Whites leaving Naini Tal. The mother, Mary Jane, was in it too, for in 1911 she had bought Grassmere, apart from owning Gurney House and Clifton. By 1909, Corbett had acquired three more estates, Aberfoyle, Hutton Hall and Mount Pleasant, bringing in an annual rental income of Rs 15,000. Matthews and Co. ran the business from Newbery Lodge on the Mall. By 1927, the family had owned or sold at least ten houses in Naini Tal.

After his return from Mokameh Ghat in 1919 Corbett took over the hardware shop and the business. He also branched out as the pioneer stockbroker of the town after 1929. When he left India, he liquidated his own shareholdings worth Rs 40,000.

Mary Matthews died in 1911. She is buried in Lucknow. Corbett was the executor of her will. She gave away all she had to the Catholic mission at Jeolikote, apart from the family portraits, medals and her trinkets which went to a nephew, Frederick Ryon of the Burma Forest Service. Poor thing, she had only Rs 60 to be distributed equally to her two servants, both Lal Mony by name, and her washerwoman. A nurse who was looking after her got the fare to go wherever she wanted to in India.

The business thrived till Corbett's mother died in 1924. She was the big drive behind it. 'Money was her god', a Corbett nephew commented. After Mary Doyle's death in 1940, Maggie and Corbett lost interest in the business. As the mortgage was cleared, there was no more buying of houses, but only selling. One of the last he sold was Mount Pleasant in 1934. He lived there for years, in this lovely house tucked away in an oak forest with a fantastic view and its own wildlife—kakar and pheasant—zealously guarded by its owner. The shop closed first and then the houses went. By 1940 Corbett had sold all and moved into Gurney House again, the house his mother had built.

The annual administration report of the Municipal Board for the year ended 31 March 1920 reports Corbett's return to city politics. Capt. J.E. Corbett, IARO, it says, was appointed to fill the place of Dr Pandya, who resigned on 2 April 1919. The same report mentions a contribution: 'Capt. J.E. Corbett, IARO, placed Rs 7,300 at the disposal of His Honour the Lieutenant-Governor and expressed a wish that this money should be expended for the benefit of Naini Tal. A bandstand on the Flats, estimated to cost Rs 4,000, is nearly complete and it is suggested that the balance be spent in providing a soldiers' reading room. The Board and the public are deeply indebted to Capt. Corbett for his generosity.' This sum was perhaps his entire war bounty.

Naini Tal was then a small town with fewer than 17,000 people. The same year Corbett rose in the civic hierarchy from ordinary member to vice-chairman on the death of the incumbent, J.R. Muirhead, on 12 September. A Board resolution mentions the acquisition of 'an energetic and efficient successor'.

A Board resolution of 1921 says: 'The public service rendered by Capt. J.E. Corbett will be brought to the notice of the Government.' Apparently this referred to the bandstand which 'Capt. Corbett has so generously provided for the municipality'. The year was an active one for the new councillor. He attended eleven of the twelve sittings of the Board. The Board increased the house tax that year from 9 to 10 per cent. A laboratory was set up for the bacteriological and chemical analysis of drinking water. Land for a burning ghat below the Bhowali road was also acquired.

Corbett became senior vice-chairman in 1923. That year, at his instance, 'an amendment prohibiting fishing in the lake during the night between the hours of 9 p.m. and 4 a.m. was made in the bylaws for the protection of fish in the Naini Tal lake'. He attended ten out of twelve sittings of the Board. He continued as senior vice-chairman till 1926. The report for 1928 mentions his attending only two out of twelve meetings and the 1929 report three out of ten.

In 1931, we find Corbett promoted to a Major in the Indian Army Reserve of Officers and heading a committee to 'reduce expenditure', anticipating a fall in general revenues because of the general depression. In 1933, bylaws were framed for using push bicycles in the town and steps built at the Flats to 'give it an appearance of a stadium'. Corbett regularly attended sports fixtures here and never missed a hockey match when in town.

The report for 1934 states:

Certain amendments were proposed by Maj. Corbett to the bylaws for the protection of fish in the Naini Tal lake and published for objections. Their final adoption is under consideration of the Board. On the motion of Maj. Corbett, the Board by its resolution No. 20, dated April 12, 1933, resolved that the Naini Tal municipality be and is hereby constituted into a bird sanctuary and that the killing of all wild birds within the municipal limits is forbidden subject to rules to be framed by a committee appointed for the purpose. Rules were framed under the Wild Birds Protection Act, 1887, and submitted to the Government for confirmation, but the Government have pointed out that the above act has since been repealed by the Wild Birds and Animals Protection Act, 1912, and does not provide for the making of such rules.

In 1934, Maj. Corbett's amendments to the bylaws for the protection of fish in the lake were adopted. With these amendments 'three-fourths of the machans have now been reserved for professional fishermen and they are not allowed to fish at any other place. The monthly rent of the machans has also been reduced from Rs 2 to Re 1.'

Corbett now turned to another project dear to his heart, saving the town forest. The report for the year ended 31 March 1937 mentions his introducing a motion to 'the effect that pack goats be licensed as they do a lot of damage in the municipal forests and private compounds'. Bylaws were framed accordingly and they came into force on 1 March 1937.

The next year he took up the cause of the overworked mules and ponies of the town. 'On the suggestion of Maj. Corbett and after considering the objection filed by the owners of pack ponies and donkeys, an amendment was made in the bylaws

---

for the regulation of pack donkeys, pack mules, or pack ponies kept or plying for hire to the effect that there shall be at least one driver for every four animals and that no such animal will be allowed to work on a Friday except in the months of July and August.'

The global economic depression now hit the town with the UP Government discontinuing its hill exodus as an economy measure. In 1938, a Publicity and Development Department was started in Naini Tal. It issued a tourist guide and a brochure to attract tourists.

In 1939 Corbett introduced a motion 'to the effect that fishing from the bank about 100 feet northwest of the drain near the soldiers' boatshed to the intake chamber of the Talli Tal latrine water supply below the junction of the roads leading to the Chase and the M.E. Church be prohibited'. The Board agreed.

Much more interesting are the minutes of the Public Works Committee which Corbett headed. The committee, among other things, sanctioned applications from citizens to fell trees in their house compounds. The committee was rather strict, and when it met on 21 July 1924 it rejected an application from the Rev. J.N. Hollister to cut enough branches from trees below the mission sanatorium to enable the occupants 'to see the tower clock on Humphrey High School'. While allowing another applicant to fell trees it insisted 'that new trees be planted in place of the old ones' in the compound and 'trees watched to see that they live'. A third applicant was allowed to cut some trees on condition that he planted three deodar saplings for each tree cut.

So conscious of the looks of the town were the councillors of Naini Tal of that time that regular rules were laid down in 1936 for the protection of trees in the municipal forest as well as in private compounds. 'Any person desiring to cut trees or to lop any branch thereof within the municipal limits shall apply to the Board for sanction to do so', the rules said. The applicant had also to state the reasons for his proposed action, the number of trees standing, whether any had been cut in the past year and, if so, how many saplings had been planted to replace them in the particular area. The committee, the sanctioning authority, could at any time revoke its permit before the actual cutting if a personal inspection showed that the grounds for felling were not sound.

Corbett's second term on the Board started with the first meeting he attended on 22 December 1919. From 1920 till 1923 he was vice-chairman, and then senior vice-chairman of the Board till 1926. He also presided over meetings of the Finance Committee, Toll and Tax Committee and Public Works Committee. He attended his last meeting of the Board on 27 August 1940 and resigned with effect from 4 October 1940. As 'Hitler's war' had started he had other plans to fulfil.

What were the civic problems of Naini Tal in the 1930s? They were the same as those of any town in the plains, but the White man took extra pains here to keep the town's natural surroundings intact from vandalism. Corbett's contribution as a councillor covered this aspect particularly.

Old issues of the *Naini Tal Gazette in which the Lake Zephyr is Incorporated*, a 'social weekly and advertiser', throw some light on these problems, particularly the popular column by T.G. Gill, a former Philander Smith schoolmaster turned journalist and a friend of Corbett. His column of 25 July 1936, under 'Zephyr Notes', said:

As I am very much interested in our city Board, I must suggest something for the good of 'Our Fathers'. It is all well to attend meetings, garden parties occasionally and so on, but what good does this do for the public? Our Fathers should take on duties, such as looking after the market, but must not yield to the temptation of Adam of old when apples were about. Others might see to the cleanliness of the bazaars, the coolie menace . . . while the agile ones may chase the galloping horses. 'Eyesore' inspection might be taken on by others, while one or two might see to the dandies and rickshaws, so as to prevent strikes. The ponies should have their teeth examined. This I am positive could easily be done. Lavender and rose drains might also be inspected. The Harijan member should certainly look to the interest of his 'bhai bund' and stand them a tea occasionally. A couple of strong members should be told to keep an eye on the fuel and charcoal depots and see that bits and pieces are not supplied. If this is done, I am sure good will result. The chairman, MOH [Municipal Officer of Health] and a European member have been on the warpath among the aerated water factories. Others should do likewise. Is Naini to be like Allahabad and other places? A cow has now taken to wandering about the roads and bazaar. Is this allowed?

T.G. Gill, whose elder brother, H.W., was for years the secretary of the Municipal Board, lived in Strawberry Lodge, close to Gurney House. Corbett was a frequent visitor. T.G. died at Bhowali in 1959, just short of ninety-two, where he lived with a daughter. He was blind by then and was never able to publish his history of Naini Tal.

'Why do you find fault all the time?' his daughter, Mrs G.M. Hainsworth, asked him once. 'It's my job, girl', he said. He wrote under the pen-name Pahari, sparing none in his hard-hitting sallies.

Corbett, alas, was not able to devote much time to civic affairs between 1922 and 1936. Robert Bellairs, a friend we meet in *The Temple Tiger*, was a local White like Corbett, and also a volunteer officer in World War I. Perhaps they struck up a friendship in the army or stoked it then. In 1919, at the base of Trishul, Maj. Bellairs discussed his problems with Capt. Corbett—his father was determined to disinherit him. The father, James George Stevenson—he changed his name from Bellairs—was a planter who owned two thriving tea estates, Chaukori and Berinag, in the interior of Kumaon. Stevenson sold the first, but when he announced the sale of Berinag, Corbett, as a property agent, dutifully stepped in and bought it outright for his friend, according to a local legend. The friend would not have it free from him, so a clerk of Matthews & Co. came in handy to manage the tea estate on a lease of Rs 4,000 a year.

Corbett soon sold Berinag and with the ready cash agreed to become a partner of Percy Wyndham, who had bought an estate on the slopes of Kilimanjaro in Tanganyika. Wyndham, as Commissioner of Kumaon, could not find much time to attend to his estate across the Arabian Sea, and so its management was left to Corbett. Corbett now installed Robert Bellairs there and himself oscillated between Tanganyika and India between 1922 and 1936, spending six months a year in each country. This explains the thin attendance at the Naini Tal civic Board meetings of the period. According to *Current Biography*, he owned a share in the Tanganyika estate as late as 1946. The game on the slopes of Kilimanjaro—buffalo, rhino, impala, eland, and greater and lesser kudu—were added attractions for him. (The attic in Gurney House is still cluttered with some of his African trophies, he did not take them back to Africa.) Corbett supervised the irrigation of the farm, and its products were so good that the government used to buy up its entire production of maize and coffee. Maggie has said:

In 1922, Mr Wyndham, a personal friend, suggested to Jim that they should go together to Tanganyika, where Mr Wyndham had a coffee farm on the slopes of Mt Kilimanjaro. Jim was so taken with the place that when Mr Wyndham suggested they become partners Jim eagerly agreed. He built a house there of which he was very proud, as he laid most of the bricks himself.

Owing to the commitments in India—neither Jim nor Mr Wyndham could remain in Tanganyika for many months at a time—Maj. Bellairs, who had been a tea planter in India, joined the Kikafu estate and managed it until 1947. During this period Jim went over annually for 14 years, and it was then he told me that when the time came for him to retire it would be to one of the silent places of the earth.[2]

The Kikafu farm was on the western side of the river after which it was named. It lies north of the Moshi-Arusha road, about twelve miles from Moshi. It was perhaps confiscated German property and bought by Wyndham after World War I from the Custodian of Enemy Property. The farm extended over 1,450 acres at an altitude of 3,500 feet.

[2] Ruby Beyts' notes.

W.H. Baldwin, the oldest planter of the area and the owner of a coffee estate from 1924 and a cattle farm later, said of the farm and its owners:

They had an additional area also on the Kingori on the west side of the Sanya Plains east of Mt Meru. About 1931, a young friend of theirs, Shackles, opened this last area for maize, but the slump had started and he sold the crop for 1.50 [shillings] per bag of 100 kg and then packed up.

I met Corbett only once in Moshi at a sports meeting when Sir Donald Cameron visited the district.

The Kikafu estate was covered in fairly heavy bush and coffee planting went ahead up to about 150 acres. About 1933, development was carried on with maize and this area was extended. Maize grew very well there.

The first house on the estate was in common with all early buildings on farms, of mud and wattle, with a high-pitched grass roof. Later, they built a very pleasant substantial cedar house with a ground floor and a first floor. Bellairs and Wyndham each had a bedroom on the upper floor. Bellairs also had his den on the ground floor. Bellairs and Wyndham took a great interest in all local farming affairs, but I do not think Wyndham had much to do with farm management. Wyndham had some interests in tea in Kenya at Kericho, I think. When the summer came round in Scotland, he used to spend the summer there, possibly on one of the west coast islands. Although I cannot remember any particular hobbies, he might well have done a lot of fishing. Twice Bellairs and Wyndham came to us for the day. They always liked to arrive for breakfast. Once we suggested they come for Christmas. Wyndham said he had not spent Christmas under a roof for thirty-five years and would like to continue the tradition.

Bellairs was very keen on shooting when in India, although I don't think he did very much here. He came out with me twice after buffalo and rhino, which were plentiful in those days.

I cannot recall the last time I saw Wyndham and am almost certain he was not here at the outbreak of the 1939 war.

At the outbreak of the war in 1939, the German owners of estates were put under arrest and the non-Nazi types used as assistants on coffee farms at Oldeani. On Kilimanjaro, the enemy estates were formed into groups and supervised by the few British and Greek planters, who in addition to managing their own estates

supervised the groups. Bellairs acted as a group manager for a year
or two. About 1947, Kikafu changed hands and finally came into
the possession of a new farmer from Kenya, who after a few years
sold the farm to a neighbouring estate. However, last October on
the 22nd [1973] the estate came under nationalization.

After selling Kikafu, Bellairs joined a partnership with Mr and
Mrs Marr on a small cattle farm of about 1,000 acres. After a few
years, all three went to Rhodesia, where Bellairs died also. I think
he is buried at Livingstone.

As for Corbett's other bits of property, the fishing lodge
at Bhim Tal was built after 1906 in more solvent days.
Corbett, oddly enough, never stayed in it. It was rented out.
When he came to fish at Bhim Tal, he preferred to stay at
the dak bungalow. The keeper of his fishing lodge was Khim
Singh, a former employee of the Naini Tal Yacht Club, who
made friends with Corbett when he was a boy by providing
him with tackle when he fished for tiddlers in the Naini Tal
lake. According to Chatur Singh, the son of Khim Singh,
the father also kept titbits for Corbett to eat when he dropped
in after school. Khim Singh was allowed to farm the land
which went with this house, called Gurney Lodge. The house
was later sold because of a series of troublesome tenants.
When it was sold, in true Corbett tradition the keeper was
given a bit of land free to build his own house at the edge of
the estate.

According to Maggie,

Jim purchased the village of Choti Haldwani in 1917.[3] The place
was practically derelict, with most of the houses in ruins and the
fields completely overgrown with grass and weeds. He very soon
set to work to remedy this sorry state of affairs by fencing in the
village little by little as his means permitted and later substituting
the wire fence with a masonry wall 5 feet 10 inches high. Jim
personally assisted in the clearing of the land, spending many hours
cutting bush and moving heavy rocks.

Later he built a cement waterway, thereby replacing the old

[3] A doubtful date, for by this year a wire fence surrounding the village was
ready.

rough channel through which there had been so much seepage that the lower end of the village received only a small trickle of water, quite inadequate for its many needs.

In the surrounding boundary walls, gates were made to provide the villagers with easy entrances and exits for their cattle and carts. As means permitted, Jim had new houses built and old houses renovated. News of all this renovation quickly spread, and people soon came forward to take up land, and gradually the village developed into one of the best in that part of the country.

Often as I walked along its paths as the sun went down with the evening light on the ripening corn and the blue hills in the background, I would think there could not be a more beautiful village in the world. . . .

He encouraged the villagers to grow their own fruit and vegetables, not only that they should have a more varied diet but also that they should be able to sell their surplus in the market. From his estate in Tanganyika, Jim brought banana plants of the best varieties, and from the Botanical Gardens in Saharanpur he brought grapevines and fruit trees.

Apart from all that Jim did to help his tenants in Choti Haldwani, he also encouraged the inhabitants in the district to grow better maize. This he did by distributing a cigarette tin full of seed, which he had brought from Tanganyika, to each man and woman as they came to do their business in the Naini Tal market. The people were anxious to have the seed in order to grow bigger and better bhuttas than ever before, and soon produced maize cobs as much as 14 inches long in place of the very ordinary ones they had been growing up to this time.[4]

[4] Ruby Beyts' notes.

6 'Carpet Sahib'

'We are not stealing Kalwa [a bullock], are we?'
'N—o,' the small girl answered indignantly, turning
her big brown eyes on Corbett.
'To whom does it belong?'
'To my father.'
'And where are we taking him?'
'To my uncle.'[1]

ORBETT WAS after the Mukteswar maneater, one of his first three, and he was escorting a little girl leading an unwilling bullock on a road where 'men were afraid to walk except when in large parties, and on which in four hours I had not seen another human being.' The banter was in the local dialect.

Baptized Edward James and buried as such, Corbett was 'Carpet Sahib' the do-gooder of the maneater legend and the patriarch of Kaladhungi. He was Jim to his patrons, friends and fans. He ran his bank account at Naini Tal as Captain and later Major Edward James Corbett, VD. This was the volunteer officer's decoration. As a city father and house agent of Naini Tal, he signed his papers as James Edward. He never could stick to one name. These together provide a vignette of the man.

Well before the turn of the century, a major impact of India on its rulers was the foisting on them of its own much-maligned caste system. The highest in the White pecking order were those Britons serving in India who had

---

[1] *The Temple Tiger*, p. 45.

their home links intact. The next were the Domiciled Europeans, who had adopted the country but retained their racial purity. The last were the Anglo-Indians (Eurasians), who had lost caste with the injection of local blood. On the top rung of the ladder sat the Britons of the Central Services, the Indian Civil Service downwards. These 'White Brahmins' would mix socially neither with the Domiciled nor with the Anglo-Indians.

As those on the top rung struggled to keep their identity intact with exclusiveness, the two groups on the lower rungs tried desperately to climb up. The Domiciled were also in the unenviable position of losing caste if they chose an Anglo-Indian bride. Even the average Indian was aware of the importance of the pigment order, and his treatment of persons belonging to these groups was tempered by this knowledge.

The White Brahmin was tolerant of the 'native', but the Domiciled and the Anglo-Indian, though in love with their adopted country, disliked the 'native' because of the graded shade of deference shown by them. In order to rise on the social ladder the Domiciled and Anglo-Indian had to be more British than the British. They had to prove it all the time with their devotion to Britain, the King-Emperor and the Empire, particularly in times of trouble. Corbett's errands of mercy and his efforts to excel as a hunter have to be seen in this light too. For while accepting the district officer's request to rid an area of a maneater, or while chasing the bandit Sultana, he was serving Britain and the Empire as well. He was born in a Domiciled English family with a standing of two generations.

In *The British Betrayal in India* the Anglo-Indian leader Frank Anthony claimed Corbett was an Anglo-Indian in terms of the word's new usage. When confronted for proof of this, he had none. Corbett was clear about it though. Perhaps aware that the community would filch his name some day, he wrote in *The Man-Eating Leopard of Rudraprayag*: 'We were the only Whites in the district.' Ibbotson was another. In *Jungle Lore*, Corbett goes out of his way to identify as an Anglo-Indian a railway station master who sold trained birds. In the same book comes a statement about a 'mad Englishman' (himself) dragging a leopard not quite dead by its tail. The London *Times* obituary notice called Corbett a European. The reader may take this as an unnecessary digression, but it is necessary to understand the White caste system that operated then and gave a schizoid psyche to the Domiciled Europeans and Anglo-Indians. They were repudiated by the White Brahmin as well as the 'native'.

Perhaps the caste system also kept the brother and at least two sisters away from marriage. If Corbett had entered the army as a career, he would not have got a commission with his lowly education. As a child he oscillated between two poles: his English school education and the koi hai White upbringing at Naini Tal and the long winters he spent with the 'natives' in his village. That was true of his adult life as well.

He lived like a patriarch in his Choti Haldwani village. The house he built or renovated on land he had bought, conveniently situated on a road trijunction, was open to all in distress at all hours. One came for a letter of recommendation to an official for a favour, another with a complaint against an underling of the Raj, and yet another escorted a sick man for medicine. With its apothecary background, the family ran a dispensary for the sick. Till her death, Mary Doyle presided over it. After her, Maggie and Corbett took over. All ailments, from pneumonia to sore eyes, were treated. The family kept abreast of developments in modern medicine and in the World War II years sulpha drugs were in free use.

The villagers from far and wide came to Jim for medical aid, and had the utmost confidence in his treatment. Malarial cases were the most frequent, and their constitutions were so weakened by this scourge that during the winter months they were unable to stand up to the cold, with the result that they developed pneumonia and all sorts of bronchial trouble. A very common cause of earache came from a tick making its way into the inner ear. This was easily

cured by inserting a few drops of olive oil into the affected part.
Women often came with bad injuries caused by falling from high
branches of trees whilst cutting leaves with which they fed their
cattle. There were also cases of dog bite, and on one occasion a
woman had the muscles of her leg torn out while separating two
cats who were fighting. There were two cement platforms under
big mango trees in the garden, which formed the surgery, and on
these platforms the patients were treated.

When the time came for Jim to return to Naini Tal, the people
would say: 'What are we to do while you are away?' Jim would then
tell them of simple remedies such as a hot lemon and honey drink
for a cold, or a poultice of wholemeal for a boil.[2]

Corbett wanted his village to be a model. He parcelled the
land into forty holdings, built irrigation channels, distributed
vegetable seed and encouraged his tenants to grow fruit. The
long wall he built over ten years to protect the crops of those
tenants in not-so-solvent circumstances is still intact. While
the grain ripened, he assiduously shot marauding hordes of
parakeets and sat nightly over the potato patches for pig and
porcupine. When a townsman would not stop his nightly
tomcatting forays into his village despite warnings, Corbett
caught him one night by the pyjama strings and thrashed
him. The elders of the town of Kaladhungi, which is half-
Hindu and half-Muslim, always turned to him as an arbiter
when communal riots broke out.

Christmas was a big day in the Corbett household, with
open house to the village and the town of Kaladhungi. Braces
of peafowl and jungle-fowl, shot a day earlier, went to his
friends at Naini Tal and the house got ready to receive adults,
children and the mothers who escorted them. Ram Singh,
his devoted servant, was the bearer of the message to the
schoolmaster inviting the children. Corbett collected a big
assortment of toys, trinkets and handkerchiefs for the annual
sports and Maggie presented the prizes.

She recalls that it was a

village treat, supposedly for the children of our village. But there

[2] Ruby Beyts' notes.

was no age limit, and there would be babies in arms, young men
and women, and greyhaired grandparents. Others in the outlying
villages soon got to hear of the annual entertainment and began to
join in, until the numbers increased to hundreds, and all were
welcome.

The treat was timed to start at 3 p.m., but long before that, on
the great day, from early in the morning a steady trickle of guests
started to arrive. Attired in their best and gayest apparel, they were
content to wait, chattering and laughing with their friends until
zero hour arrived.

The school children in the charge of a master would line up in
front of the house and shout 'Garge Panchim Badshah ki Jai'
followed by 'Corbett Sahib ki Jai',[3] and then march off in a neat
line to the nearby field where the entertainment was due to take
place. The party commenced with all our guests sitting on the
ground in an enormous ring, and our men—who had to be of very
high caste—would then go round with big baskets distributing
sweets. These had been especially ordered from the bazaar, and the
bania[4] had been up at dawn preparing them as Indian sweets have
to be absolutely fresh to be worth eating. After the sweets, fruit
would go round, oranges and bananas being chief favourites.

The feast over, games began and these were many and varied.
People of all ages took part. I think the game the children enjoyed
most of all was that in which a blindfolded child had to pierce with
a stick a paper bag filled to the brim with sweets, and suspended
from a horizontal pole. The fun continued until the sun began to
sink low in the west, when after many expressions of gratitude for
such a lovely day everyone would return home, tired but happy.
The village people had so few pleasures that they appreciated to
the full a simple entertainment such as this and it afforded them
much to talk over and laugh about during their leisure hours.[5]

One winter during World War II, after Corbett had been
invalided out of the army, the star attraction at the children's
party was a rag dummy of Hitler. The boys were given sticks
and asked to hit the dummy on the run. The one who hit it
on the head got a handkerchief, and the one who hit it on
the leg only a whistle.

[3] Glory to George V. Glory to Corbett Sahib.
[4] The right word is halwai.
[5] Ruby Beyts' notes.

Once a touring district magistrate and his wife who were staying in the forest rest-house opposite were invited to the party. The magistrate's wife graciously produced her own massive Christmas cake. But it was not acceptable to the Hindu children. So Maggie solved the problem by segregating the Muslim children and distributing it to them.

Then there were children's days in the forest. Corbett loved to go bird shooting with them. Several patches of scrub would be beaten by the boys and, as the day's bag of peafowl, junglefowl, hare and an occasional deer or pig was collected, a package of parched gram and jaggery was produced for the boys. Corbett insisted that game should be shared by all. On a lean day he would go to the extent of forgoing his own share.

To Kaladhungi and the surrounding forest he had a zoo approach, zealously guarding game. As a self-styled game warden he enforced shooting laws and even preached sports ethics to a party of hunters whom he caught leaving a wounded tiger in the vicinity. People treated him with awe, for Carpet Sahib even knew the Viceroy!

This position and confidence sometimes led to brushes with authority, as when Corbett sent a man one day to protest against the killing of a leopard by a forest officer at the rest-house. This former officer of the Indian Forest Service, recalled Corbett as being a typical 'hoity-toity White' who patronized the poor Indian but was intolerant of the better-placed one, particularly if he was a high government servant. Corbett had sent his man to protest with the message: 'You have killed my leopard.' Back came the reply: 'I did not see a dog collar and did not know it was yours.' Corbett always treated the area around Kaladhungi as his own private preserve.

When Corbett caught a friend from the town poaching the story was different. Ram Datt Sati, a clothier, and a friend were once drawn to a chital hind belling in a thicket after wandering for hours without luck. As they got to gun range they were greeted with a chuckle as Corbett emerged. 'Why don't you ask me when you want game?' he said. Crestfallen, they both accompanied the hunter to the point where the road to the bazaar and Corbett's village parted. At the parting of the ways Corbett emptied his own game bag and presented both with one jungle-fowl apiece. 'One should not go home empty-handed', he said.

He believed in educating people the hard way. Panua, the lad who took over as his shikari after the death of his father Mothi, carelessly rested his rifle one day on the sandbed of the Baur river. Corbett picked up the rifle, and gently dusted the bolt and the locking device with his handkerchief. Half way to the house, he pointed to a round boulder in the riverbed and asked Panua to carry it home. He needed it to make some medicine, he said. Poor Panua trustingly carried it home huffing and sweating. When he dropped the stone at the house, there was a quiet reproof: 'One does not rest a rifle on sand.'

The biggest tiger shoots Kaladhungi saw were fixed for Linlithgow. On one occasion sixteen elephants were present. Several machans had been built in trees. Corbett's villagers then basked in the limelight, in close proximity to the highest in the land. They alone knew the local forest and were generally in charge of the details. Panwan Gusain, the son of Dhanwan, in recounting his youthful experiences said that early in the morning, when the last instructions were given to his select band from the village, it was dinned into their ears: 'Remember, the Bara Lat Sahib [Viceroy] will be the first to shoot. If the tiger is not shot, my name will be mud—not only here but also in Vilayat [England].' With this the men climbed the trees either to act as stops in the beat or as gunbearers and companions to the elders and the women in the party.

The beat started. The elephants moved in a phalanx and the stops in trees from both sides let out bloodcurdling screams and rattled tin cans. Two tigers broke cover far out from the Viceroy and loped towards the long line of machans made for the guests. Silence ruled again. Panwan, who had helped a General up a tree and had been asked to keep an eye on him, saw the tigers, and his charge, the General, lifting his rifle. Panwan, realizing that the Viceroy would not have the first shot, shouted 'sher, sher' to the consternation of all, especially the General, who had his rifle beaded on one by now. Hearing the shout, the tigers changed direction and re-entered the grass patch in the direction of the Viceroy.

The General now had his rifle pointing at Panwan on the other tree. This was not a situation Panwan had bargained for and, as the shot rang out from the Viceroy's machan, Panwan slipped down his tree and headed for Corbett's near by. Now it was Corbett railing at him: 'Get up a tree fast, you paji. You will be mauled by a wounded tiger.' The equivalent of 'scoundrel' in Hindustani, *paji* was Corbett's favourite expression when irritated. It has some endearing undertones as well.

But Panwan did not stop till he reached Corbett's tree and settled down in a lower fork. 'What happened?' asked Corbett. He pointed to the General in the other tree glaring at him and mumbling obscenities. Only his lips could be read from that distance.

Soon the all-clear was sounded. The elephants hauled in the tiger. The guests were helped down the trees. The General, who had needed the assistance of three men to go up, got down unassisted and headed for Corbett's tree. Panwan, seeing him coming, cowered behind Corbett on the ground, fearing physical violence. Corbett tried to pacify the General, but when this did not work, he raised his voice. What passed between the two Panwan did not comprehend for he knew no English. He only remembered a string of abuse sprinkled with the word 'bastard'. When the General left, there was a big smile for Panwan and the endearing paji again. Panwan came in for more glares from the General in the remaining three days he was in camp.

The viceregal shoots also gave Corbett a chance to slight the local contractors, businessmen and other busy bees. While leaving, the Viceroy had once graciously offered to shake hands with those who had made the arrangements. Old residents of the town remember that he ignored them all. Corbett's own tenants and the Forest Department staff were the only ones allowed the privilege.

How did Corbett come to know Linlithgow?

Soon after his arrival in India the Viceroy, Lord Linlithgow, whilst on a visit to the Governor of the United Provinces, was lent a copy of his little book, *Jungle Stories*, and was so interested in it that he expressed a wish to possess a copy for himself. This wish was conveyed to Jim, who sent Lord Linlithgow a copy. I think it was the reading of this little book that led to the Viceroy's desire to visit the scene of some of the stories, for in the following spring Jim received a message from one of the viceregal staff asking him if we could suggest a place in which the Viceroy could spend a holiday and get some shooting. Jim suggested Kaladhungi, and we were greatly honoured by invitations to house Lord and Lady Linlithgow on several occasions and also to visit them in Simla. We very much enjoyed this visit. Jim especially enjoyed his games of tennis and billiards with Lord Linlithgow. During our visit, the Maharaja of Patiala invited the viceregal party to a very enjoyable bird shoot in his state. Later on we were invited to Viceroy's House in Delhi. The last occasion was a farewell visit on the eve of Lord and Lady Linlithgow's departure from India.[6]

Corbett also organized a tiger shoot for Linlithgow's successor, Lord Wavell. Wavell's *Journal*, edited by Penderel Moon, for 1 January 1947 reads:

Jim Corbett . . . was running the shoot with Yakub Khan and some of the Bodyguard. His talk on tigers and jungle life is of extraordinary interest, and I wish I could have had more of it. He has rather pessimistic views on the future of tigers; he put the present tiger population of India at 3,000–4,000 (I was rather surprised at the smallness of this estimate) and that in many parts of India tigers will become almost extinct in the next 10 or 15 years; his chief reason is that Indian politicians are no sportsmen and tigers have no votes, while the right to a gun licence will go with a vote.

Naini Tal was for years the headquarters of the Eastern Command, and many a General sought Corbett's help to bag

[6] Ruby Beyts' notes.

a tiger or two. There was a lot of bandobast in these shoots but little killing. There was a joke about one General who could not sleep at night when he heard a tiger. The next day he called his ADC and had the camp shifted to a place where he could sleep peacefully.

Till he rubbed shoulders with royalty in later years in Kenya, organizing the Linlithgow shoots were Corbett's biggest social triumphs. Five tigers were shot in the first hunt, four in classic textbook pattern. Only the last one caused some anxious moments. Linlithgow, Viceroy between 1936 and 1943, visited Kaladhungi and the neighbourhood at least three times to hunt and fish. Lord Hailey, Governor of the province, also came to shoot. So did Hallett, the next incumbent.

At Narain's at Naini Tal, the bookshop which supplied the Corbetts with their newspapers, the proprietor remembered Corbett as a gentle, self-effacing man who would wait his turn patiently even if a small boy was buying a pencil. At his bank, the first call he would make was on the young ledger clerk. 'No, I must talk to you first, my boy', he would insist, though he collected the money from the manager's room.

One evening, at his village gate, seeing a frightened little boy running towards the Kaladhungi bazaar, he asked him what the matter was. 'It's getting dark, and I have to reach the bazaar', the boy said. 'Where are you from?' The boy said he was from Bhim Tal. 'Whose son?' Of Maula Baksha, the dak bungalow keeper, the boy said. That was an old friend of his angling days in Bhim Tal, and the son was therefore escorted right up to the bazaar, a mile away. On parting, the boy was given Rs 5.

On one of the annual winter exoduses to Kaladhungi, when the luggage was unloaded, one bundle which contained the heavier quilts had a gaping hole and a burn mark, the handiwork of a careless muleteer who had flicked a lighted cigarette on it. Maggie, the more practical of the two, was angry. But Corbett did not forget to slip his usual bakshish to the muleteer while Maggie was occupied with something else.

I have often wondered about Corbett's compassion for the blind. His first book was dedicated to them. But he was tough on one blind man. After he had bought his estate at Choti Haldwani, Corbett had the unpleasant task of evicting a squatter, an old Muslim woman who raised goats for mutton. She is still remembered in the village when a healthy, well-fed goat is about. 'Like Sherroo's goat', they say. She had a blind son, Tanne, who after the mother's death became a beggar and a charge on the town. When Corbett was in the village there were standing instructions to the kitchen that something should always be kept aside for Tanne. Tanne, who had been nursing a grouse against Corbett over his mother's eviction, was leaning against the Corbett bungalow gate and abusing the sahibs. Corbett had arrived the same morning, but the blind beggar was ignorant of this. As the words he used were filthy, Tanne got a good hiding.

A journalist[7] trailing the Corbett legend in the Kumaon countryside found memories of the hunter intact even in 1970. Matela is a village some forty miles from Naini Tal which Corbett visited several times in the hunt for the Chowgarh tigress, and where he was once summoned to take care of a cattle-lifting tiger. The 79-year-old patriarch of Matela warmed up the minute Carpet Sahib was mentioned. 'Carpet Sahib was God. The goddess appeared to him in person. He only killed the flesh-eating animals, never the defenceless ones . . . ' (This was only true of Corbett's later years.)

'He wasn't a government servant, but like Ramsay he ruled the hearts of the people of Kumaon. He was the peacemaker when people quarrelled. His clean white handkerchief came out if he met a child with a runny nose', the patriarch reminisced. 'He would care for the sick, sitting with them for hours, and give money to take the very sick to the hospital at Naini Tal. He was a simple man. Often, he slept on the

[7] Kailash Sah in *Saptahik Hindustan*, 13 December 1970.

piled grass in my courtyard while passing through and ate whatever was cooked.'

His wife added: 'He loved the local food. He respected Hindu sentiments and never entered a temple courtyard without removing his shoes.'

The patriarch remembered that Corbett was a great one for not contracting obligations. If he ate in a house or accepted a glass of tea, he would quietly place some money in a child's hand before leaving. If a child was not around, he would leave an eight-anna bit on the threshold of the house or in a niche in the wall. He was conscious of the abject poverty in the countryside and maintained that horticulture could revolutionize the economy of the hills. The orchards at Okhalkanda were planted with the apple and peach trees he imported for the people from Australia.

Though himself not a reward hunter, Corbett wanted others' acts of heroism and loyalty rewarded. One man he wanted honoured with a collection was the Nepali servant of the headman of nearby Lamachaur, who would not allow his master to be insulted by Sultana's men and paid the price for it. He was shot dead by dacoits. This man's dependants could not be traced, so the project was abandoned.

Another act of heroism Corbett wanted noticed was that of two basket-makers who, while out to secure a permit for bamboos, encountered a feeding tiger in high grass. As the tiger attacked the man at the rear, the one in front dragged his companion to safety with the menacing tiger growling behind them. This is the story of Haria and Narwa as told in *My India*.

Corbett tried to get Haria some recognition, but red tape came in the way. It was pointed out that as there were no independent witnesses nothing could be done. Corbett toyed with the idea for a time of appealing to King George VI himself, but gave up because World War II had broken out and the King would certainly have more important things to worry about. Corbett hated red tape and thought it was one of the factors responsible for the exit of the Raj. His best administrators were Anderson of the Tarai and Ramsay of Kumaon who, while touring, distributed justice on the spot after hearing both sides, without the assistance of lawyers.

Corbett took pleasure in flaunting his favourite weather-beaten hunting coat with a dozen patches. To a villager who commented on its 'disgraceful' condition, he said: 'Look, I am not that poor, but I want the people to know that it is all right if they have the same.'

All heroes collect a vast, colourful legend. Corbett was no exception. One was a curse that the hundredth tiger he shot would be his last. If he killed one after the ninety-ninth, he would be mauled and killed thereafter. This legend grew when the sportsman left the rifle and took to the camera. For why should a man discard the rifle if he was not afraid of the curse? And how many tigers and leopards did he kill? According to a villager of Kaladhungi, Corbett told him once that he had killed some 250 leopards and about fifty tigers. Another legend was that he could converse with animals. That was true if the talking was limited to copying a few animal and bird calls and not holding a regular conversation. Once, while calling a leopard, Corbett found himself looking up the rifle barrel of a hunter who did not know he was about.

'And then Carpet Sahib threw his hat at the tiger and as he jumped at it shot him' was the most popular story. This was partly true, for on occasions he did use his hat to break the charge of a wounded animal in high grass. He found the method useful. He waved his hat at an animal he had spared to let it know of his harmless intentions. Also, he thought it was 'not cricket to molest an animal that has provided entertainment'.

Another legend was that, dressed as a woman, he 'attracted the maneaters and killed them either with a sickle or an axe'. This was not quite correct. Corbett himself had this to say: 'All I have ever done in the matter of alteration of dress has been to borrow a sari and with it draped round me cut grass, or climbed into trees and cut leaves, and in no case has the ruse proved successful; though on two occasions—to my knowledge—maneaters have stalked the tree I was on, taking cover on one occasion behind a rock and on the other behind a fallen tree, and giving me no opportunity of shooting them.'[8]

As for fearlessness, Corbett writes truthfully of the night of terror while waiting for his first maneater: 'When the night wind agitated the branches, and the shadows moved, I saw a dozen tigers advancing on me, and bitterly regretted the impulse that had induced me to place myself at the maneater's mercy. I lacked the courage to return to the village and admit I was too frightened to carry out my self-imposed task, and with teeth chattering, as much from fear as from cold, I sat out the long night.'[9]

Later, he wrote: 'If the greatest happiness one can experience is the sudden cessation of great pain, then the second greatest happiness is undoubtedly the sudden cessation of great fear.'[10]

[8] *Man-Eaters of Kumaon*, p. 27.
[9] Ibid, p. 18.
[10] Ibid., p. 246.

7 Snakes, Spooks

Jim Corbett prefers to wear shorts
Jim Corbett was a bachelor
Jim Corbett must kill a snake first
then he is sure to kill the man-eater
for he was a bachelor
Jim Corbett lived with his sister all his life
for he was a bachelor
he killed man-eaters
because he loved the created world
he deeply revered His Majesty the King
he loved Indians too . . . [1]

SHALL I cite the raising of a child in the predominantly
Hindu hills of UP or the many close shaves Corbett had
while out after maneaters to explain his belief in the
occult? While engaged in this dangerous pastime, we find
him making offerings at a temple whenever one was conveniently situated, or his men making trips to them either
for good luck or as thanksgiving. The priest of the rock
temple of Pakhan Devi, just above the lake at Naini Tal, was
a lifelong friend of Corbett; Corbett even allowed a Hindu
astrologer to cast a horoscope for him. This is in the archives
of an astrological magazine. He kept open house on Hindu
festivals except for the rather rowdy Holi, which he could
not stomach. On Divali he sent trays of sweets to the girls
of Wellesley at Naini Tal. The brother and sister wanted to
be cremated if conditions permitted. In his later years, beef

[1] Excerpt from a poem by Vilas Sarang, *Modern Indian Poetry in English*,
Writers Workshop, Calcutta, 1969.

was taboo in the Kaladhungi house out of deference to local sentiment.

Corbett considered Fridays bad for starting journeys and hated all snakes. Over the years, he had found that killing a snake always brought him luck. He killed a hamadryad with two stones while out after the Kanda maneater. He noticed a ratsnake crossing his path when he was leaving Garhwal after his first failure with the maneater of Rudraprayag. The success there immediately followed the killing of a snake by Ibbotson.

About this, Corbett says:

I do not know if sportsmen are more superstitious than the rest of mankind, but I do know that they take their superstitions very seriously. One of my friends invariably takes five cartridges, never more and never less, when he goes after big game, and another as invariably takes seven cartridges. Another, who incidentally was the best-known big-game hunter sportsman in Northern India, never started the winter shooting season without first killing a mahseer. My own private superstition concerns snakes. When after maneaters I have a deep-rooted conviction that, however much I may try, all my efforts will be unavailing until I have first killed a snake.[2]

Incidentally, the snake is a powerful male libido symbol and one wonders what Corbett was really trying to kill. It is interesting to examine three symbols in Corbett's life to study his ascetic aspect. If a man, as far as we know, has no sex life, he is bound to show some projection. The gun is a well-known pre-Freudian phallic symbol and the quarry—the cat tribe—represents the female libido. And if it is not the gentle pussycat but a ferocious wild animal—*Panthera tigris* in our context—this would represent the ferocious wild aspect of the same, threatening the celibate 'White sadhu'. A sadhu is supposed to be off sex. So if Corbett took care of the snake first (phallic symbol) he was sure to defeat the maneater (threat of the female, the devourer of masculinity).

[2] *Man-Eaters of Kumaon*, p. 171.

Even the title of his first book is intriguing: in a psychic idiom, the triumphant record of an ascetic fighting his shadow side. I wonder if the roots of asceticism were in the canal-bank assignment—when the nighties billowed, he was asked to look the other way—with a possible association of sex with dirt. If so, this trauma would keep a man away from women, seeking the safety of the wilderness—there are no women there—and unconsciously pitting his wits against the ferocious aspect of woman. I also wonder whether the Tsavo man too was an ascetic.[3]

The White sadhu was very much in evidence when he wrote of a night spent in the gorge of the Sharada river and sighting mysterious lights in the vicinity of the rock shrine of Punyagiri. He was hunting the Talla Des maneater. This he took as a favour 'accorded to me and to the men with me, because I was on a mission to the hillfolk over whom the goddess watches'.[4] This was not a will-o'-the-wisp, as the lights were of a uniform size and not affected by the wind. A letter to the editor or an article Corbett wrote in 1930, his first literary venture perhaps, raised quite a controversy round the mystery at that time. Even Hailey, with whom he was fishing in the river next year, wanted to check on it.

Corbett had an eerie experience one night at the Champawat dak bungalow while after his first maneater. The tale of the bungalow, which he promised to write some day, is perhaps lying somewhere among the Corbett papers and is worth digging up. The tahsildar of Champawat, who had offered to stay with him that night, finally walked down to his house at night with one lantern and one lone attendant for company in maneater country. Left to himself in the dak bungalow, something 'beyond the laws of nature', as Corbett puts it, occurred—but he never published the tale.

Corbett was sensitive to ghosts all his life. There was a night he spent in a raja's house in Naini Tal district about

[3] J.H. Patterson, *Man-Eaters of Tsavo.*
[4] *The Temple Tiger*, p. 127.

which he remained enigmatic. This incident has been vouched for by a former ICS officer who was in the house the same night. World War II was on, and the two, on an assignment for the government, were offered the hospitality of the raja's summer house. But they were warned that one particular room should be left alone. When Corbett was told about this, he insisted on sleeping in it. Neither the chowki-dar's protest nor his friend's warning had any effect. Midnight came, and nothing happened. The ICS man was asleep, and so it seemed was Corbett. About 2 a.m. there was a distur-bance in Corbett's room. As the ICS man opened the con-necting door, Corbett rushed in, panting for breath.

He spent the rest of the night in the ICS man's room. Next morning, over breakfast, the man asked Corbett what had happened. Corbett left the table abruptly and asked never to be reminded of the night. This mystery remains unex-plained.

About Corbett's series of failures to kill the Temple Tiger of Debidhura, one can only quote the priest of the temple: 'I have no objection, Sahib, to your trying to shoot this tiger, but neither you nor anyone else will ever succeed in killing it.'[5] Corbett could not, and hoped that 'in the fullness of time this old warrior, like an old soldier, just faded away.'

Equally mysterious were the blood-curdling cries he heard in the deserted village of Thak while after the maneater of that name. He was in a tree sitting over a buffalo. As the moon came up, a sambar with young and a kakar came to graze. Then came the cry 'ar-ar-ar' from the village, the cry of a man in despair. The kakar and the sambar heard it and dashed away. Next morning, when Corbett closely ques-tioned the headman of Thak about the maneater's last victim a fortnight earlier, he confirmed that the man had cried out three times while being carried away. And the rendering he gave of the agonized cry was a fairly close one to what Corbett had now heard.

[5] *The Temple Tiger*, p. 8.

About these incidents Corbett himself says:

But though I claim I am not superstitious I can give no explanation for the experience I met with at the bungalow while hunting the Champawat tiger, and the scream I heard coming from the deserted Thak village. Nor can I give any explanation for my repeated failures while engaged in one of the most interesting tiger hunts I have ever indulged in . . .

The last reference is to the Temple Tiger. Elsewhere he writes:

Superstition, I am convinced, is a mental complaint similar to measles in that it attacks an individual or a community while leaving others immune.[6]

While hunting the Chowgarh tigress, a man who had just been warned to be careful was carried away by her. Corbett very philosophically wrote: 'When Atropos, who snips the threads of life, misses one thread she cuts another, and we who do not know why one thread is missed and another cut, call it Fate, Kismet, or what we will.' This tigress was following Corbett and his men when she took the man.

I suppose a biographer has to dig up some facts about his subject's love life. But on this, as on many other aspects of his life, Corbett decided to be silent. The furthest he has gone in describing Indian womanhood is his 'Queen of the Village' in *My India*. He writes of a meal taken from a brass plate in the house of the woman concerned, and the scramble that followed among the daughters to clean the empty plate of the White sadhu. Corbett, aware of caste prejudice in such matters, wanted to clean it himself. The daughters of the house had their way and assured him that washing it would not make them lose caste. 'Her hair, snow white now, was raven black when I first knew her, and her cheeks, which in those far-off days had a bloom on them . . . was the "Village Queen"', he wrote of the mother.

[6] *The Temple Tiger*, p. 5.

An interesting find has been a fixed deposit receipt for Rs 4,180 in the name of Aditya Binai Kumari issued by the Fyzabad branch of the Allahabad Bank. Checked at Fyzabad, it was found that the money was given by Corbett to the Third Princess of Balrampur, a former princely state of UP. The year was 1928 and Corbett was fifty-two. We do not know why the money was given, for the princess is dead and the family will not talk. Perhaps it was an act of compassion. If so, it fits the White sadhu image. But why a fixed deposit? Many of the legacies in the Corbett will are also fixed deposits. I suppose he met the princess in one of the many tiger hunts he arranged for the governors of the province. The Balrampur family, which once kept one of the biggest herds of elephants in the province, provided some to the hunting camp.

Maggie appeared to be taking all Corbett's attention after the death of his mother. Jim was known as the 'jam sandwich' of the family, the sister on one side and the mother on the other. Maggie lived continuously with him from 1943 till the end. She looked after him through sickness and adversity. She kept house for him. For her he killed one of his last tigers, for it was operating in an area where she took her evening constitutional. She brewed his tea at the crack of dawn when he went out to shoot, and kept the hot water ready for his evening bath. Maggie went fishing with him to the Baur river and took long walks in the forest with him when he went out with gun and dog. The Thak maneater was supposed to be his last mission in deference to her wishes. She did not want him away from home so much.

Maggie loved fishing and ventured with Corbett on trips further afield than the Baur river. About one trip to the lake district of Kumaon she says:

In the autumn of 1915, Kumaon experienced a very severe earth-quake—the most horrifying that we had ever known. Jim and I were in a boat fishing on Sat Tal lake, about 12 miles from Naini Tal. Suddenly the boat began to quiver in a most unaccountable way, and the first thought that flashed across my mind was that the quivering was due to a volcanic eruption. The Kumaon lakes were thought to have been formed in this way. The quivering rapidly increased, becoming more and more violent until I thought the boat must be upset. The fish, being alarmed by the disturbance in the water, were jumping up on all sides, and a huge snake went swimming across the lake at great speed. At the same time there was a tremendous report and rocks came crashing down the hillside bringing enormous trees in their wake. All this was very alarming and I suggested we might get off the water, but Jim said we were safer where we were. After a while the noise and the disturbance ceased and all was quiet once more. A few days afterwards, Jim happened to be passing through some villages of Kumaon where he found that numbers of houses had collapsed and were in ruins due to the earthquake.

Jim's next experience of an earthquake was when he was sitting up in a tree in Kaladhungi, hoping to get a picture of a leopard. Suddenly the tree in which he was perched began to wave about, and Jim wondered whether it was the leopard trying to get at him from behind or whether it was a big snake crawling up the tree. On looking around, however, he saw the other trees behaving in a similar manner, although there was no wind, and later he discovered that this was the tail-end of the disastrous Bihar earthquake in which thousands of people perished.

Another day as we were crossing the Boar [Baur] bridge, on our way home from an evening walk in the jungle, the creaking of the metal bridge told us that an earthquake was in progress. This was not severe, however, and we just stood where we were whilst the shock lasted.[7]

An old lady of Naini Tal who knew Maggie well ventured the comment that Maggie was very possessive and would not let Corbett marry. At Naini Tal, she occupied herself first as a piano teacher and later doing social service. She was on the governing body of All Saints' School and was the acting general secretary of the Naini Tal District Girl Guides' Association in 1932.

One of the last wishes of the sister was to see a proper biography of her brother written. She turned to Cumberlege for it and gave him long talks about the family, but Cumberlege did not attempt a regular one for the facts supplied

[7] Ruby Beyts' notes.

were inadequate. But he wrote an excellent introduction to the World's Classics edition of *Man-Eaters of Kumaon* and *The Temple Tiger*, published in 1960.

Disappointed here, Maggie next turned to a friend, Ruby Beyts. She dictated her some thirteen pages of notes in 1957, with instructions to write them up 'one day after she died'. Ruby Beyts' husband, G.H.B. Beyts, a former Brigadier of the Indian Army, Gen. Thomas Corbett (a Corbett nephew) and Jim Corbett shared a farm at Mweiga in Kenya. Jim was a sleeping partner. Ruby Beyts once asked Maggie why she and her brother had remained celibate. Maggie said their lives had been so bound together that they never considered marriage.

The Periodical, a house journal of Oxford University Press, wrote about Maggie in its spring issue of 1964 to mark her death: 'She was as devoted to her brother as he was to her. The books . . . were his; but her part in their creation was a key one. She looked after her brother, she made the home to which he returned from his long days in the jungles of Kumaon, she was the first to hear the stories and reminiscences which were to be read by thousands in many lands. And she read the proofs. Together, they appeared an almost incongruous pair: Jim very tall, gentle, soft-footed; Maggie very small, smiling and silent. But they were very alike in their courage and their modesty. Maggie is mentioned many times in the books; but she was as self-effacing in her life as her brother was in the jungles of North India. Her many surviving friends will remember her, in the words of *The Times* as "the most unselfish person they have ever known".' Maggie missed her ninetieth birthday by three weeks.

When confronted with the question as to why he did not marry, Corbett told Marjorie Clough: 'It has been my privilege . . . no, I have had the honour to make a home for the best mother and sister in the world.'[8] Corbett also said that Maggie had devoted all her life to spoiling him.

What did Corbett look like? There are still many people

[8] *Current Biography*, 1946 edition

alive, albeit increasingly ageing, who remember him. People (such as the publisher of this book) who were children in Naini Tal in the 1940s recall Maggie and Jim out on their evening walks together. Jim is remembered by them as a bear-like, kindly-faced man who wore a felt hat. Occasional-ly, he would entertain (and sometimes terrify) them by im-itating the calls of wild animals. Maggie seemed altogether severer to them, and less approachable—but she is remem-bered by one 'boy' (now in his late-fifties) for having fed him a pastry when he strayed into the grounds of Gurney House in pursuit of a bouncing rubber ball.

To Marjorie Clough he was 'an erect, ruddy mustachioed six-footer with twinkling Irish eyes that laugh and are sad all at once. Though quite bald on top, his hair is very much white and abundant.' This was the portrait of the hunter in 1942. Geoffrey Cumberlege wrote: 'Jim was tall and spare and kept to the end of his life the figure of a young man. No one failed to notice the blueness of his eyes, his shy and compassionate expression which easily and frequently changed to a warm smile. Simple, modest, friendly, quiet in manner and a delight-ful talker, he was a man to whom everyone was attracted. Many have felt his saintly quality and none would deny that he was a great man.'[9]

And what did Maggie think of her brother? 'Jim had no patience with self-pity or anything that savoured of it. He always made the best of things and enjoyed life to the full. He never seemed hurried or flustered, but always found time to listen to the troubles of others. Never careless of his appearance, however shabby and old his clothes, he looked neat and tidy in them. Grace of movement, one of his most notable characteristics, was perhaps partly due to his having lived so much amongst wild animals, whose movements are always so graceful.'[10]

[9] Introduction to World's Classics edition of *Man-Eaters of Kumaon and The Temple Tiger*.
[10] Ruby Beyts' notes.

8 Hunter

. . . And then I felt a gentle pull on the blackthorn
shoots I was holding and blessed my forethought in
having had the shoots tied to the leaning tree, for I
could not turn round to defend myself and at best the
collar of my coat and my hat were poor protection. No
question now that I was dealing with a maneater, and
a very determined maneater at that. Finding that he
could not climb over the thorns, the leopard, after his
initial pull, had now got the butt ends of the shoots
between his teeth and was jerking them violently, pull-
ing me hard against the trunk of the tree. And now the
last of the daylight faded out of the sky and the leopard,
who did all his human killing in the dark, was in his
element and I was out of mine, for in the dark a human
being is the most helpless of all animals and—speaking
for myself—his courage is at its lowest ebb. Having
killed 400 human beings at night, the leopard was quite
unafraid of me, as was evident from the fact that while
tugging at the shoots, he was growling loud enough to
be heard by the men anxiously listening in the village.[1]

SCOFFERS, MOSTLY not-so-famous brother hunters, have
questioned how so many maneating tigers and leopards
were concentrated in only a small part of the country,
Kumaon. This region, at the base of the Himalaya in UP,
comprising the foothills of the Bhabar and the level areas of
the Tarai, was a broad tract of dense forest up to the turn of
the century and teemed with game. For ages this had been

[1] *The Temple Tiger*, p. 84.

tigerland. So long as a tiger was in his prime and could hold his own as far as a mate and territory went, he had the best in the world.

But with age and declining vigour, he had to give way to younger animals. The weak had to leave the territory in the struggle for survival. Driven out of his own territory, he would make a desperate bid to hold another bit of territory. But if an intruder, he was driven away by stronger rivals, and ultimately out of tigerland.

This dispossessed creature could now make one of two moves. He could migrate to the settled areas in the south or to the hill forests in the north. Open country without cover is not the habitat of the tiger, and a settled area provides a bigger conflict with humanity in terms of cattle lifted. A better alternative was the hill forest. But here the tiger found himself in alien surroundings. The rough terrain meant a bigger effort to procure food. He missed the easier catches of the Tarai forest and started living off cattle. This led to brushes with farmers armed with muzzle loaders. Sooner or later, he would be wounded and unable to hunt even cattle, and would then turn to human beings as nutriment in dire necessity. So year after year the infirm moved north out of tigerland to end up as cattle-lifters and, when wounded, as potential maneaters.

A big inducement for a tiger to move north was the herds of buffaloes and cows returning to the hills from the Tarai forest in early summer. In the winter months the hillmen of Kumaon move to the foothills with their herds in search of pasture. With summer they return, and a tiger driven out of his traditional hunting grounds logically followed the long cattle trails, hoping to get a straggler or two. The cattle caravans shortened and petered out as people reached their villages. A day then came when the tiger found himself stranded without a vision of easy meat on the hoof. He had to make new adjustments in an alien setting.

When he agreed to rid an area of a maneater, Corbett laid down two conditions to the district officers: the reward offered to kill the animal should be withdrawn, and so should the other hunters assigned the task. He did not like the role of a White hunter, nor having armed men around him. He took on the White hunter role unconsciously sometimes by organizing off and on the shoots of high-ups, governors of the province and at least two Viceroys, with collectors and generals thrown in. The one exception he made for armed company was A.W. Ibbotson, with whom he hunted the Rudraprayag, Thak and Chuka maneaters for a time.

But benefits from hunting accrued to him all the same in the form of an immense legend that grew round him as a saviour, and a grateful government piled honours on him. These included an honorary magistrateship, the Kaisar-i-Hind gold medal, the OBE and the CIE. The last title came in 1946. Two other signal honours granted to him were the Freedom of the Forests and the renaming after him of India's first national park by the UP Government. The first of these was a privilege that only one person had enjoyed before him, according to Corbett.

There is, however, no reference in the Forest Department manual to this right. When questioned, senior forest officers ventured the opinion that what Corbett perhaps meant was that he was treated like the 'exempted category' of forest officers who paid no shooting fees and were allowed to shoot tigers in the first fortnight of the month of the tiger season. Others said it could mean a free life permit to shoot anywhere he wanted. Hailey called it the right to enter any reserved forest.

Organizing hunts for high-ups brought Corbett into close contact with top bureaucrats and celebrities and made him one of the most influential men in the province in the 1930s and 1940s.

Before the ban on tiger hunting came, as each state took action in 1970 and 1971 (wildlife was incongruously a wholly state subject till Act No 53 of 1972[2] came into force),

[2] The Wild Life Protection Act, 1972.

1. *Corbett's house in Kaladhungi, now a museum*

2. *The author on the aqueduct that carries the Baur canal to Kaladhungi bazaar; the ruins of Arundel in the background*

3. *Family group, Naini Tal (c. 1900). From left to right: Mary Doyle; a brother (unidentified); Jim's mother; Jim; Maggie*

4. *Head of the Champawat maneater:*
'the upper and lower canine teeth on the right side of her mouth
were broken . . . the cause of her becoming a maneater' (Corbett)

5. *The Rudraprayag leopard: 'his chin resting on the rim of the hole and*
his eyes half-closed . . . peacefully sleeping his long last sleep' (Corbett)

6. *Corbett with the Bachelor of Powalgarh*

7. *Corbett holding a 50 lb mahseer:*
'The fish of my dreams', caught in a well-stocked submontane river

8. *Jim Corbett, c. 1944*

9. *With a bird perched on his palm: Corbett in Nyeri*

10. Tree Tops Hotel, as Corbett knew it

11. The Baden-Powell suite in Outspan Hotel
which the Corbetts occupied

12. The graves of Corbett's parents: Sukha Tal cemetry, Naini Tal

13. Corbett's grave in Nyeri, Kenya

irreparable harm had been done to the future of this animal. The credit for the ban goes to enlightened world awareness of the problem of wildlife rather than to India, the biggest homeland of the tiger. The International Union for Conservation of Nature and Natural Resources (IUCN) campaigned vigorously for the tiger's protection. At its general assembly in New Delhi in 1969, the Union recommended a moratorium on tiger shooting till 'such time as censuses and ecological studies, which are in operation or proposed, are completed and reveal the correct position as regards population trends'. For a viable tiger population, it is necessary to have a contiguous area where at least 300 animals live. There is no part of India where this condition obtains.

There were two types of tiger hunters before the ban came, depending on the hunter's means and temperament. One was the bandobastwala who, by spreading a mat of money on the jungle floor, or with local influence, got his tiger driven out of the forest in a beat to within the range of his rifle on a howdah or a machan well beyond harm's way. The princes, busy-bee VIPs of all sorts who were pressed for time, and high government servants, were in this class. The hunter had only to press the trigger, the rest was done for him by others.

If the animal was only wounded, the hunter could commandeer elephants and follow the injured animal to give it the *coup de grace*. In the days of the Raj, tigers were royal sport zealously guarded for Whites and princes. By courtesy, gazetted officers of the Forest Department could also shoot them. But woe betide the ordinary man who transgressed this order of things.

The solo hunter who stalked tigers on foot belonged to another class. He was the braver of the two, for he took a legitimate risk, sometimes even a 50:50 chance. Corbett belonged to this class, though when the necessity came he was not against planting buffaloes and goats in the forest and sitting over them to secure a kill. One must be a Sherlock Holmes of the wilds to be able to stalk a tiger on foot. The art comes after mastering the jungle telegraph, the knowledge of what every animal or bird call means, and the capacity to read the jungle floor, what a footmark or imprint means. This knowledge has to be backed with a sound eye, ear and nose.

In defence of this form of shooting, Corbett says: 'When shooting on foot, it is very much easier to kill an animal outright than when shooting down on it from a machan, or from the back of an elephant. For one thing, when wounded animals have to be followed up on foot, chance shots are not indulged in, and for another, the vital parts are more accessible when shooting on the same level as the animal than when shooting down on it.'[3]

The tiger-stalker is also a naturalist who, having pitted his wits against it, acquires a respect for Stripes. To him, it ceases to be the 'bloodthirsty animal' it is called by those unaware of the laws of the jungle.

For most of Corbett's hunting record one must read *Man-Eaters of Kumaon*, *The Man-Eating Leopard of Rudraprayag* and *The Temple Tiger* together. Except for some excellent digressions, one being the story of his dog Robin, and of two fishing interludes on the Ramganga and the Mandakini, the books give a connected narrative of his exploits against the maneaters he killed as well as others which were killed for sport or for other reasons.

Corbett's active period of maneater hunting was spread over 32 years, from 1907 to 1938, in a life span of eighty. There were twelve maneating tigers and leopards responsible for killing over 1,500 people in the villages of the hill districts of Garhwal, Almora and Naini Tal. Corbett shot his first maneater in 1907, when he was thirty-one. The last, the marauder of the Ladhya valley, was shot in 1946. Corbett was then over seventy.

The Thak maneater, a tigress lured to its doom by Corbett giving a mating call, was to have been the last of this category that he was to hunt, because of family pressures and advancing age. Ibbotson was with him part of the time. This one

[3] *Man-Eaters of Kumaon*, p. 49

was shot at pointblank range from a precarious hold on a cliff. The operation nearly ended in disaster when he slipped, but he was saved by his men. This was in 1938. But he returned later to the same valley to kill his last maneater.

The Pipal Pani tiger, a celebrity of Kaladhungi first seen as a cub and whose career the hunter had followed for fifteen years, was similarly called and shot under the mistaken notion that he would be a menace to the area because of a wound. But this was not a maneater.

The Kanda maneater, about which an appeal was sent to 'Carbitt Sahib' by the villagers of Garhwal in February 1933, was shot under dramatic circumstances from a low perch in a tree with the tiger growling at the hunter. This one, after being wounded, was also called close, it did not give the hunter much of a chance, but he killed it finally.

The Mohan maneater of the Kosi valley, which operated from Kakrighat to Garjia and was known for the low moans it emitted while moving, was killed after the hunter had recovered from an attack of laryngitis. This one, which had gorged itself on a buffalo used as bait, was caught sleeping on a ledge. Corbett regretted it was not given a 'sporting chance', even if it was a maneater. It had a festering wound caused by embedded porcupine quills.

The Bachelor of Powalgarh, not a maneater, was also called and killed. It was shot as a trophy. Between 1920 and 1930, when it met its end, hundreds of sportsmen had tried their luck. It was of record size, measuring 10 feet 7 inches over the curves.

The Chowgarh tigress and her cub were responsible for 64 human lives in a five-year reign of terror which ended in April 1930. Trailing them, Corbett spent three nights in trees, one of them close to a family of noisy Himalayan bears feasting on kafal (*Myrica esculenta*) berries. He sat over a kill, a cow, and by mistake shot its cub but not the tigress. This error cost twelve more human lives before she too met her end. The hunt for her had once to be abandoned after a month, but not before the hunter had proved his prowess with an axe in dispatching a wounded Himalayan bear. The following February, he returned to the scene, killed two tigers over a dead cow and finally met the maneater in a ravine. The tigress had followed him and his men. It was a tricky, almost impossible shot at close range, the left hand cupping two nightjar eggs gathered on the way for his collection. The eggs were restored to the rock nest, for they had brought him luck.

The usual post-mortem findings made at the time of skinning explained why this tigress had maimed more men than she had killed. Her claws were broken, and a canine tooth as well as the front teeth were worn down to the bone. Deprived of help from her cub, she had become a greater menace.

The Champawat maneater, responsible for 436 kills, had been driven out of Nepal to eastern Kumaon. This was Corbett's first maneater but not of Kumaon, for several were operating before that, even close to Naini Tal in the 1840s.

As he visited the sites of its human kills, 'dreading and hoping to meet him', Corbett spent the first night squatting on the ground against a tree. The first lessons in what not to do when a maneater is around were learnt. A beat was organized, the first for a maneater, and the animal shot. The lower and upper canines of the tigress were broken, the result of a gunshot wound, and that accounted for her becoming a maneater. This was in 1907.

'The Temple Tiger' is the story of a charmed tiger and Corbett's inexplicable failure to shoot it. It was a cattle-lifter. The account is enlivened with a blood-curdling interlude, a fight between the tiger and a brave Himalayan bear which had tried to dispossess the tiger of its kill, with disastrous consequences to itself. Corbett could not shoot the tiger but killed the wounded bear.

The Mukteswar maneater, which had the misfortune of losing an eye and had an added disability after receiving some fifty quills in an encounter with a porcupine, was responsible for twenty-four lives when the call for aid came to Corbett.

The first attempt to shoot it over a kill, a bullock, failed. It was a dark, wet night and Corbett had to rely entirely on his sense of hearing. The tigress hovered around the tree in which Corbett was, growling till the rain started. Later, after a beat, he shot it in what looked like a headlong charge.

The Panar maneater, a leopard responsible for 400 lives from 1905, was shot in 1910, the same year that the Mukteswar tigress met her end. While out after the leopard Corbett inadvertently spent a night in a leper's living quarters. Another time a leopard bounded off with his dinner, a joint of mutton. Sitting in a low tree over a live goat, the hunter had the eerie experience of the quarry trying to climb his tree. Luckily, the trunk had been made secure with a bundle of thorny bushes tied with rope. Then the leopard went for the goat and killed it. The hunter got in a shot with his double-barrelled shotgun. Perhaps unwisely, he allowed the villagers to help him down the tree with the wounded leopard prowling about. They came with lighted pinewood faggots and he got in another shot at the leopard.

The Chuka maneater, which Corbett hunted with Ibbotson, now lovingly called Ibby, was also a tiger caught sleeping, with only its rear showing. The first shot incapacitated it and the second killed it. Its right canine was found broken, and several pellets of buckshot were taken out of the carcass. Travelling up to the haunts of the tiger, the hunter and his friends, the Ibbotsons, did some good fishing in the Sharada.

The Talla Des maneaters, a tigress and her two cubs, were apparently shot all in a row in a terrific show of marksmanship. But the wounded tigress got away and was cornered only after five days of hard tracking. These three were responsible for 150 human kills. The tigress, known as the Lame One, had twenty porcupine quills in her right leg and shoulder.

The story of the hunt, deliberately withheld for years, was the only one which needed a long explanatory memorandum with place names and a witness. This was so because brother tiger hunters had started accusing Corbett of exaggeration, about the Chowgarh hunt for one.

Two miles ahead of Rudraprayag, on the Lucknow-Lhasa
route, as the Border Roads Organization fondly calls the
pilgrim road to the shrine of Badrinath, the men who look
after the road have put up a signboard at Gulab Rai reading:
'Have you read *The Man-Eating Leopard of Rudraprayag* by
Jim Corbett? It is at this spot that the leopard was shot.' For
years the animal depicted on the signboard carried stripes
and not spots, a sad commentary on Indian natural history.

The Rudraprayag leopard, which operated along the pilgrim
route between 1918 and 1926, deserved a separate book for its
uncanny wiles and daring. It had got into the habit of entering
houses at night and dragging its victims out. Leopards being
scavengers, this one acquired a taste for human flesh after the
1918 influenza epidemic, which led to careless disposal of the
dead because of a shortage of manpower. It made its first
human kill on 9 June 1918, and its last on 14 April 1926, and
altogether took at least 125 human lives. The hunt was in two
stages, partly in 1925 and partly the following year. Twenty
nights were spent on the windswept tower of the Rudraprayag
suspension bridge waiting for the killer. Corbett returned to
the scene in the spring of 1926 after a series of failures.

Ibbotson, then Deputy Commissioner of the stricken district, was with him most of the time, assisting in the arrangements. As the animal was a veritable fiend, no effort, sporting
or unsporting, was spared to get him. These included poison-
ing the kills with cyanide and laying gin traps. At least once
the leopard ate the poison, with apparently no harmful effects.
On the eleventh night, perched in a mango tree at Gulab Rai,
Corbett got it while sitting over a goat as bait. This one had a
canine broken, several healed bullet wounds and one unhealed.
It was the night of 1 and 2 May. Incidentally, Corbett lost his
cigarette case that night.

In 1972, there were only a few old men alive in the district
to remember the terror of the early 1920s. One, a retired forest
guard of Kobe village, aged eighty-three, said:

There had been some maneating leopards in the area, but this one [of Rudraprayag] had wings—at least this is what we felt. Each victim was picked miles away from the previous one. From sun-down to sun-up, the local populace lived in abject terror. Even indoors in a closed room, one imagined it was crouching under the bed, lurking in a corner or silently keeping a death watch at the door. The particularly nervous ones had nightmares.

Even by day, people moved about in groups. But as the evening shadows lengthened, it was always a race for home. Few dared to go out at night, not even to attend to a call of nature. I was at Rudraprayag when the leopard was shot. All of a sudden, the tension that had held us in its grip for years vanished and one almost felt one was in a vacuum. Some doubted it was the maneater, for it was credited with supernatural powers and could not be killed. But seeing was believing. The doubters believed too when for a month peace reigned over the pilgrim route.

The killing ended a long period of terror, and it was commemorated with an annual fair at Rudraprayag, perhaps the only fair in the world connected with a leopard. This was kept up for years. Any significant event in the hills, in the absence of a written historical tradition, was kept alive in folk songs. At least four of these were still in circulation in 1972. Two of them have even been included in a locally published anthology. (See the Appendix for an English rendering of one of them.)

Mukandi Lal, barrister-at-law and Deputy Chairman of the UP Legislative Council in the 1920s, a brother hunter who had accounted for five tigers and twenty-three leopards, was a regular visitor to Naini Tal after 1924 as a member of the Council. He made friends with Corbett who, when he left for Kenya, presented him with half a dozen books, one of them Boswell's *Life of Johnson*. The MLC, who gave up shooting after his twenty-third leopard mauled and nearly killed him, had kept up pressure on the Government with regular questions in the Council about the Rudraprayag maneater. It was operating in his constituency. One of the questions was: 'How is it that when one man is murdered, the Government spends thousands of rupees to bring the murderer to book, whereas no serious attempt is being made to kill the leopard responsible for over a hundred lives?' As a visitor to Gurney House he heard at first hand some of Corbett's exploits. In his election campaign for the Legislative Council in 1926 Mukandi Lal had also sat for the leopard, without luck, in a room from where it had taken a woman.

When he skinned his maneaters, Corbett always sought a justification for killing them. Even the Rudraprayag leopard, which nearly got him at least once, does not earn a clear verdict of crime and punishment. Corbett had to write about it: its crime was 'not against the laws of nature, but against the laws of man'. The hunter always made a quick retreat from the scene before sun-up once the maneater had been skinned and the locals feasted their eyes on the carcass. He hated all fuss and being in the limelight. The only exception was with the maneater of Rudraprayag, when he stayed on—perhaps in deference to Ibbotson—to acknowledge the gratitude of the people at a bazaar reception.

To merit destruction by him in later years a tiger or leopard had to be a habitual maneater. A tiger on a fresh kill, one with cubs or one wounded would attack when disturbed. Corbett would not call them maneaters. He believed in giving the animal the benefit of the doubt at least twice before labelling it a maneater.

In later years, when he abandoned the rifle for the camera, he did not think much of his trophies. His collection was stowed away in his Naini Tal house and never displayed. Comparing the two forms of sport—wildlife photography and trophy hunting—Corbett says: 'While the photograph is of interest to all lovers of wildlife, the trophy is only of interest to the individual who acquired it.'[4] He also said that the dustbin was the ultimate destination of all trophies.

However, Corbett took his major trophies to Kenya. The skin of the Bachelor of Powalgarh was willed to Henry Z.

[4] *Man-Eaters of Kumaon*, p. 249.

Walck, then president of Oxford University Press Inc., New York. But Walck did not finally get the Bachelor, for when Maggie wrote to him after Corbett's death that it was not in good condition he agreed to accept the skin of the Thak maneater. The rest of the skins were auctioned by the executors of the will, the Standard Bank of South Africa Ltd., Nairobi, in two lots. The proceeds from the first lot went to blind Africans in Kenya, and from the second to the blind in Kumaon. Maggie sent the proceeds from the second lot, Rs 10,000, to the Governor of UP on 7 March 1959.

As for his hunting triumphs, Corbett narrates them modestly. To him it was a weary duty and 'good shooting an obligation'.[5] Closing his hunting record in *Man-Eaters of Kumaon*, he wrote: 'There have been occasions when life has hung by a thread and others when a light purse and disease resulting from exposure and strain have made the going difficult, but for all these occasions I am amply rewarded if my hunting has resulted in saving one human life.'

He could never say like one of his contemporaries: 'My dear, I shot my hundredth tiger fifteen years ago and then I stopped counting.' That was the claim of Tom Innes of Balrampur. A scion of the Hearsey family claimed a record of seventeen tigers in ten days, in the Kheri forests of UP.

What was Corbett's secret for the long innings he enjoyed as a hunter engaged in a very dangerous pastime? He was endowed with the faculty of sensing danger at the subconscious level, what in modern jargon we call ESP (extrasensory perception), and in the old as sixth sense. It is an occult faculty beyond the ken of sight, sound and smell. Apparently without rhyme or reason, he often writes about sensing imminent danger. But this was no literary trick to heighten drama, and has been the subject of a study, available at the Corbett museum, by Jack Phelan, an American doctor.

When hunting the Chowgarh tigress, Corbett wrote:

---

[5] Hailey's introduction to *Tree Tops*.

I have made mention elsewhere of the sense that warns us of impending danger, and will not labour the subject further beyond stating that this sense is a very real one and that I do not know, and therefore cannot explain, what brings it into operation. On this occasion I had neither heard nor seen the tigress, nor had I received any indication from bird or beast of her presence, and yet I knew, without any shadow of doubt, that she was lying up for me among the rocks. I had been out for many hours that day and had covered many miles of jungle with unflagging caution, but without one moment's unease, and then, on cresting the ridge, and coming in sight of the rocks, I knew they held danger for me, and this knowledge was confirmed a few minutes later.[6]

What brings it into operation is extreme tension. Primitive man had it, and those living close to nature can have it. On the conscious level, Corbett as a woodsman leaned heavily on the animal and bird calls of the jungle and the four winds to follow the movements of tigers and leopards. His first maneater, the Champawat, activated his intuition. While examining the severed leg of a victim, a girl, he first became conscious of it. 'I had forgotten all about the tigress until I suddenly felt that I was in great danger.' As he looked up raising his rifle, a bit of earth rolled down the bank, confirming the close presence of the tigress.

Again, he reveals a sixth sense when writing about the Chowgarh tigress:

I stood on the rock smoking, with the rifle in the hollow of my left arm, when all at once I became aware that the maneater had arrived. . . . In this area the tigress could not have approached without my seeing her; and as she had approached, there was only one place where she could now be, and that was behind and immediately below me. I have no doubt that the tigress, attracted . . . by the noise . . . had come to the rock, and that it was while she was looking up at me and planning her next move that I had become aware of her presence.

Tracking the Mohan maneater, it was there once more:

As I came round a bend in the road thirty yards from the

---

[6] *Man-Eaters of Kumaon*, p. 106.

overhanging rock, I suddenly, and for the first time since my arrival
. . . felt I was in danger, and that the danger that threatened me
was on the rock in front of me. For five minutes I stood perfectly
still with my eyes fixed on the upper edge of the rock, watching
for movement. . . . The fact that I had seen no movement did not
in any way reassure me—the maneater was on the rock, of that I
was sure.

The Kanda maneater provided him with the same experience. Before he spotted the tiger fifteen to twenty feet
away breaking cover, he had the same uneasy feeling. One
evening, as he clambered down a tree while hunting the
Rudraprayag leopard, he sensed that the leopard was following him. Tracks confirmed this the next morning. In later
years, Corbett coined a new term, 'jungle sensitiveness',[7] to
explain his inexplicable crossing of the road by night into red
dust, thus avoiding a tiger crouching behind a culvert, while
going out to retrieve a stag shot in the forest for the people
of his village.

[7] *Jungle Lore*, p. 168.

9 Naturalist

. . . And the last of the seven tigers passed within ten feet of the camera lens.

'What would you have done, Colonel Corbett, if it had seen and attacked you?'

'I should have thrown it a khaki cushion which I always carried in case of emergency.'

'But . . . a cushion? . . . how would that have helped?'

'A friend of mine once saved his life by throwing a rolled khaki blanket to a tiger who was about to spring at him. The tiger stopped to inspect the blanket long enough for my friend to shoot it.'

'And you hoped the cushion might help you do the same?'

'Well, I never carried a gun when I went out to photograph the animals. Only my camera . . . and the cushion.'

'Then what . . . ?'

'I hoped the tiger might be interested in the cushion long enough for me to get away.'[1]

THE DAY was 10 October 1951, at Amen House, then headquarters of Oxford University Press in London. Corbett had just finished screening his wildlife films, one of them *Seven Tigers*, and the viewers had been asked to put questions. Corbett was 'inordinately proud' of the tiger film.

After Corbett's death the films went first to the National

[1] *The Lantern*, vol. XVIII, no. 3, December 1951.

Film Archive in London and were eventually given to the British Natural History Museum, where they are now with the education section 'wound on to bobbins, about 20 of them, each length having a running time of ten minutes or so. They have not been edited, and the scenes are in random order. They are of course all black and white and silent. They are becoming rather fragile with age. About half the film was shot in India and about half in Africa.'[2]

With every hunter comes a time when he starts questioning whether it is worth his while cluttering up a house with hide and horn. Besides, seeing the decimation of wildlife over the years, he pauses and asks himself the question: Will anything be left for the coming generations? F.W. Champion, a pioneer wildlife photographer and a former forest officer of Kumaon (*With a Camera in Tiger-Land*), gave Corbett the idea of having trophies that could be shared by all. Corbett had received a 16-millimetre cine camera as a gift from a friend, Lord Strathcona, in 1928. Champion's still photography had been by night with the aid of trip wire and flashlight, but Corbett now went one better, getting his photographs in broad daylight.

For ten years he tried in vain to get decent pictures of tigers. Either it was the weather that ruined the film or plain inexperience. Finally, he decided on setting up his own jungle studio near Kaladhungi in 1938 and succeeded in drawing seven tigers to within ten to sixteen feet of the studio and filming them. To drown the whirr of the cine camera, he dammed the stream in the centre of the studio. Cascading water did the trick. On other occasions, he drowned the noise with bird and animal calls. The filming took four and a half months' hard work and countless hours of waiting at the studio, to which he repaired before first light. Before this, Corbett had been toting an 11-pound camera for years, unsuccessfully trying to get tiger pictures in broad daylight, part

[2] Courtesy, British Museum (Natural History).

of the time in the Patli Dun valley of the Ramganga which
was later to become the Corbett National Park.

Reviewing the films screened at Amen House, A.C. Ward
wrote in *The Lantern*:

But what films they were! No studio sets, no million-candlepower
lights, no makeup, no props: not even a continuity girl. No camera-
man or director but Jim Corbett; no scenery but the Indian and
African landscape, no 'stars' but leopards, tigers, elephants, hip-
popotamuses, rhinoceroses and nearly every kind of buck. The star
of stars, however, was none of these. It was a goat . . .

This was in the first spool that Col Corbett screened—mainly
about leopards. . . . When setting out to film a leopard it is, of
course, first necessary to produce the leopard. 'So I called up a
leopard', said Col Corbett, as any one of us might say 'So I rang
up for a taxi'—and, unlike some taxis we know, a leopard came.
Then the film 'cut' to a herd of browsing or nibbling goats. 'Watch
the goat on the extreme right. We shall see him again in a few
minutes.' We did. Separated from the rest he was left alone with
the leopard: which was what the leopard had played for.

After a brief exhibition of ringcraft, the leopard went for the
goat. The goat countered by meeting the leopard horns first. The
leopard stepped back to think things over, decided that its techni-
que was sound, and went for the goat again. Again those con-
founded horns! When the leopard came up for the fourth round
the goat went into action on its own account with the goatesque
equivalent of an uppercut. The contest ended in the sixth round.
As the leopard came in once more, the goat appeared to stop the
assailant in its tracks with horns and all four hoofs together. What
any properly equipped sports writer would call the 'local derby' or
'needle contest' or even 'homeric battle' was over. The leopard
threw in a spectral towel, muttered 'Goats is hell' and slunk away
to tell 'why I lost' for the next Sunday's *News of the Jungle*. The
goat, with an air of bored modesty, as though brushing off leopards
was mere kid's play, resumed its nibbling or browsing. Anyway,
that's one picture that Hollywood didn't get.

The next two films were comparatively peaceful, being concerned with the Indians' method of collecting honey from wild
bees who locate their hives in the treetops, and with the day's work
of elephants.

In the film which might be called *The Tale of the Seven Tigers* we saw the pictorial result of four months' patience and persistence by Jim Corbett. He explained that tigers are by nature solitary, preferring to roam alone, or at most in couples. He was determined to film a number of tigers in company, however. Damming a small stream, to form a pool in a spot suitable for a drinking place, he then took steps to collect the tigers. Going afield to various points of the compass where tigers were likely to be, he put down food to lure them. When this was taken, he put down further meals nearer to the pool he had made, and in this way enticed the tigers into a progressively smaller area until at length seven were together by the pool. One of the seven was an albino, its whiteness showing up queerly against the dark rocks and undergrowth. Another had the manlike trait of being in a constant bad temper about nothing in particular—growling and snarling with the venom of a politician of any party out of office. Although Col Corbett made it clear that neither the camera nor the photographer must be seen by the animals, three of those tigers appeared as lens conscious as Marlene Dietrich. They posed themselves couched on a shelf of rock with their paws (or should it be pugs?) curving negligently over the edge: three great cats.

The last film was of the birds in the Corbett garden in Kenya and of a large herd of elephants, also made in Kenya. 'During the nearly two hours that the films took to project, *only one dead animal was seen*—a maneating leopard—and Col Corbett apologized for showing even that one. . . . Though he was warmly and spontaneously thanked for his generosity in providing a unique experience, thanks seemed something of an impertinence and an irrelevance, for—as a member of the audience said privately afterwards—"Jim Corbett is the nearest to a saint that any of us is likely to see." '

According to Maggie, Jim always went unarmed to take his jungle pictures. 'I felt he was taking risks in so doing, especially during the time he spent in filming the seven tigers he had managed to get together. He always sat in the same place, about eight feet from the ground on the branch of a very small tree under which the tigers had to pass on the way to the place where they fed. So as not to disturb them, Jim took up his position very early in the morning. By putting out his hand, he could have touched the tigers on their backs as they passed below him.'[3]

Wildlife photography has its hazards too. Maggie recalls how Jim was once brought home 'in great pain and hardly aware of what he was doing or saying', having unaccountably fallen off a tree he was perched in while attempting to photograph a tiger. He was diagnosed by a doctor as having 'a broken back, severe concussion and internal haemorrhage', which, not surprisingly kept him bedridden for some months.[4]

In later years, knowing well that Stripes was on his way out, Corbett became a saviour to the dozen tigers within a radius of ten miles of his village. Whenever a delegation called to seek his assistance in killing a tiger which had turned cattle-lifter, he would open his purse-strings and offer to compensate for the cattle killed. Critics in his own village, however, imputed motives to him—he wanted them for his friends or for his camera studies.

A villager of Choti Haldwani approached Corbett once to kill a tiger which had taken his best bullock. Persuasion and compensation failed to mollify the villager. Fetching his own shotgun and shouting obscenities at Corbett's gate against the tribe of 'photographers'—that was Corbett's photography phase—the villager made a beeline for the kill. Corbett reluctantly followed and killed the tiger from a tree after calling it to the kill. The villager ruefully remembered, after the shot had been fired, that Corbett's only regret was that he had not brought the camera to take a nice picture!

This, incidentally, was one of his last tigers and 'shot after Hitler's war'. About the very last he killed, Maggie had doubted Corbett's capacity to hold a rifle steady after years of sickness during the war. So it had to be called rather close and shot through the eye. To justify the killing, Corbett said: 'It resisted all my attempts to drive it away' and 'it was difficult

---

[3] Ruby Beyts' notes.
[4] Ibid.: the accident is undated.

to replace the animals it killed because of a shortage of farm animals brought about by the war.'[5]

A lot of people today think that the preservation of wildlife and other ecological matters are newfangled ideas. If that is so, Corbett was a pioneer. He was not a killer sportsman and all his writings plead for the preservation of wildlife. What he himself destroyed, in terms of tigers, were mostly those that were dangerous to man.

On 21 May 1955, the Delhi edition of the *Statesman* reproduced a letter Corbett wrote in 1948 to an unidentified friend on the tigers of India. It read:

For 20 years I have fought in defence of wildlife and my opponents have invariably been people one would have expected to help, and not to oppose.

Men, and in some cases women, with a blood lust are always ready with an excuse—a potential maneater, possible cattle-killer and so on—and the excuses they have made are now being made by their successors.

Until India realizes that wildlife is an asset, the killing will go on.

Two years ago, Lord Wavell asked me the same question about tigers that you have done, and I told him that in my opinion there were 3,000 tigers in India. When he asked me how long I thought tigers would survive, I said that except in sanctuaries and one or two Indian states tigers would be wiped out in ten years.

That situation has nearly come about.

An earlier warning came in 1944 in the author's note in *Man-Eaters of Kumaon*, where he wrote:

There is, however, one point on which I am convinced that all sportsmen—no matter whether their point of view has been a platform on a tree, the back of an elephant, or their own feet—will agree with me, and that is, that a tiger is a largehearted gentleman with boundless courage and that when he is exterminated—as exterminated he will be unless public opinion rallies to his support—India will be the poorer by having lost the finest of her fauna.

He never sat in judgment even over the maneating tigers

[5] *Jungle Lore*, p. 49.

he shot, for he fully believed 'a maneating tiger is a tiger that has been compelled, through stress of circumstances beyond its control, to adopt a diet alien to it.'[6] Man was responsible for this mostly. A tiger left wounded and incapable of preying on its legitimate game would seek easier pastures. Sometimes it was the tiger's own folly when porcupine quills got embedded in its flesh while killing one, and old age was a third reason for its turning to maneating.

Perhaps the biggest factor that has gone against the tiger, apart from wanton killing and the encroachment on its habitat by population pressure, is the commercially oriented forest policy which believes in planting one species of trees to the exclusion of others for convenient exploitation. The eucalyptus plantations in the Tarai and the Nilgiris and the conifers in the hills illustrate this.

A plantation is not a forest. It is an ecological desert for wildlife. A natural forest is not trees alone. It is the mulch (decayed vegetation), ground herbs, tubers, undergrowth and creepers too. The exclusion of all these in favour of the tree alone has wrought havoc with nature's delicate balance. The hard truth is that a 'standardization of forests', as Corbett called the plantations, provides neither shelter nor feed to wildlife.

This is how modern forestry works to the detriment of wildlife. A patch of natural forest is selected for planting commercial timber. The trees are felled and sold as fuel. The stumps and the undergrowth are systematically burnt. Then come the pits or tractor furrows—if the terrain allows it—and the saplings are planted. Barbed wire strands then go up to protect the young plants from stray cattle and deer. Watch towers are erected for forest guards, and such deer as manage to clear some four strands of barbed wire to forage in the plantation are systematically shot. Sambar, alas, have the habit of rubbing the itch off their hides on saplings and damaging them.

[6] *Man-Eaters of Kumaon*, p. 9.

Modern forestry also demands that, for quicker growth and as protection from fire, the grass and undergrowth should be burnt regularly. The end result is evenly spaced rows of one family of trees, be it the eucalyptus, chir pine or teak, with a dry, bare forest floor which does not provide cover even to a scurrying rat. Deer may get grass here but not cover, and they desert these plantations. The undergrowth and ground vegetation, which provide the cover and supplementary feed, are not there. The pheasant and other ground feeders, who thrive on the worms that mulch produces, have nothing to eat here, for the mulch has gone. The natural forest untouched by man has all the things that sustain wildlife, a nature's garden of trees and shrubs fruiting, flowering and foliaging all the time. Alas, this forest is *kukath* (bad timber) for the forester and has to go.

The substitution of oak forest by conifer plantations in the hills is another tragedy. The worm in the oak leaf-mulch sustained the pheasant. The young leaf of the oak and the lush undergrowth sustained the deer. And the acorn sustained all the herbivora—deer, porcupine, bear and a multitude of forest birds. With the cutting down of the oak all the wildlife sustained by it is vanishing. The conifer forest with no undergrowth is hostile to wildlife.

In Corbett's Tarai, once a hospitable home for the tiger, the pattern is the same. The semal trees, whose fleshy red flowers sustained monkeys, langur and deer, which in turn sustained the tiger, have largely gone, swallowed up by a match factory at Bareilly started about eighty years ago. Vast tracts have been cleared for farming and new forest plantations, and the tiger, driven from the deerless forest, perforce goes out to feed on domestic cattle in villages along the periphery of the forest and gets shot. Unless a semblance of wilderness is restored to the forest—in other words no interference—nothing can be done to save wildlife.

The modern ecologist here faces a challenge. Can he fight plantation commercialism? Where are the biostudies of all the wildlife-sustaining trees and shrubs that season by season in an unbroken cycle provide for the needs of wildlife? What exactly is a wilderness? It is what begins where the road ends. The natural forest, undoctored by the messy hands of *Homo faber*, man the maker of things, is the friend of wildlife. Study it, restore it, sustain it, and you have the solution.

For Corbett the tiger always remained a 'largehearted gentleman with boundless courage'. He had reason to reach this endearing conclusion, for how else could one explain that two children, one of two and the other of three, lost for seventy-seven hours in Kaladhungi were rescued safe and sound, with not even a scratch, in a forest which to Corbett's 'certain knowledge'[7] held five tigers, eight leopards, a family of four sloth bears, two Himalayan black bears and a number of hyenas?

Hailey, who was a frequent hunting and angling companion of Corbett in the 1930s, writes of delegations of villagers visiting their camp and asking Corbett to rid them of a tiger turned maneater or cattle-lifter. 'But the rubric that Corbett applied to the inquisition which was now opened was strict, however friendly and considerate in its terms. It was no use for them to plead their losses in cattle or goats. The tiger was lord of the jungle and must have its dues. Not until he himself was convinced that a tiger had been killing human beings, not by chance or in anger, but because it sought them as food, would he agree to come to their help', he wrote.[8]

What exactly turned Corbett into a naturalist? According to the Rev. A.G. Atkins,[9] it happened one day on a duck shoot. In the 1930s, Atkins was the pastor of the Union Church at Naini Tal for two summers. This was the church of Philander Smith College and its sister institution, Wellesley. One evening, after Corbett had screened his first tiger

---

[7] *My India*, p. 67.

[8] Hailey's introduction to *Tree Tops*.

[9] He is better known for his translation into English of Tulsi Das's *Ram Charit Manas*, a *Hindustan Times* publication. His wife, Lois Rockey, was a close friend and girl guide companion of Maggie.

film and given his wildlife lecture, the pastor walked Corbett half way home to the lake from PSC. The road is all downhill and the two chatted. After some talk, the priest came to the point and asked him what made a hunter a photographer.

Here is the story of the 'conversion', as the priest called it:

He [Corbett] had always been fond of shikar in the ordinary sense of the term, going out for hunting or shooting with not much thought of anything else but the fun and sport of it. He was known as a skilled jungle man and was often asked to lead parties out for a good shoot. One day he was out with three military officers in one of the lake and river areas of North India. They came upon a large batch of waterfowl, literally thousands of them. The officers began shooting; they went on and on, following and killing their game till they had killed over 300. They could not possibly carry them away for any use; it was simply unrestrained slaughter for the crude pleasure of it. Said Jim: 'That sickened me and opened my eyes to what ordinary uninhibited hunting and shooting meant. I resolved from that time that I would use my jungle lore for a different kind of shooting, and in that way I began to take photographs of wild animals and jungle life. It requires much more of my skill and gives me an even greater thrill to get good pictures of my animals than when I used to hunt just to kill.'[10]

With the arrival of Hailey as Governor of UP in 1931 (this was his second term), Corbett the naturalist became a bit more articulate. An Association for the Preservation of Game in UP was formed with the Governor as its patron and Corbett and Hasan Abid Jafry as honorary secretaries. The association also brought out a journal, *Indian Wild Life*, to which the late E.P. Gee, the planter-naturalist, was an early contributor. Its aim was to 'awaken public interest in the preservation of wildlife and to take such steps as might be possible to save it from extinction.' The first issue of the monthly, priced 8 annas (half a rupee), appeared in July 1936. *The Bombay Natural History Society Journal*, Vol. 39, carried a full-page advertisement of this official organ of the Association, and also of the All-India Conference for the Preservation of Wild Life, of which the

[10] *The Hindustan Times*, Sunday Magazine, 14 August 1956.

patron was Sir Harry Haig. The Association became ineffective when World War II broke out, but Corbett was a regular visitor to Government House when Hailey was in Naini Tal. He had avoided the hustlefussabad of Government Houses so far, but Hailey was a friend, and Sir Maurice Hallett, Hailey's successor, also befriended Corbett.

Jafry, a barrister, was the political secretary of the Raja of Mahmudabad. The Association for the Preservation of Game in UP was affiliated to the All-India Sportsmen's Brotherhood, of which Jafry was also honorary secretary. The Association secured land on lease in Muhalla Purwa Ali Mirza at Lucknow on nominal payment, and the lease deed was confirmed on 8 January 1946. There was a proposal to have a building with a hall named after Hallett.

Addressing the Association at Lucknow on 5 August 1934, Hailey remarked: 'I have been much struck by the reception given to the lectures which Major Corbett has delivered; he has the advantage that he bears a reputation not only beyond compare and above approach as a sportsman, but as one who has a real love and respect for animal life.'

Catch them young, they say. Corbett now started lecturing on wildlife at Naini Tal. At Wellesley, the girls looked forward to the yearly visit of Corbett and Maggie. He usually wore shorts and shirt and a pullover. Maggie was installed on the dais and Corbett would lecture on his favourite subject, the jungle telegraph. A tiger is coming, he would announce, and then mimic a series of bird calls—the jungle babbler, drongo, peafowl—and then the animal calls—the langur, barking deer, chital and sambar. These produced a solo effect perforce, for the human soundbox has its limitations mimicking a jungle cacophony or the racket raised by frightened langur. The warning call of the deer tribe is solitary. The muntjak barks, the chital pooks or bells and the sambar ponks. The calls would change with the tiger's activities. Now, it is in cover, now moving, now stalking, and now sleeping, Corbett would announce, varying the intonations.

He would build up the climax with a tiger's growl, first

subdued and then full-throated. The atmosphere for this last
bit of performance was built up by putting out the lights.
Before it happened, he would dramatically announce: 'Anyone with a weak heart may go now.' No one ever left, and
squeals and giggles followed. All the Naini Tal boys' schools
also had the benefit of this annual performance. On Hailey's
suggestion he also lectured at the schools and colleges of
Lucknow.

At Kaladhungi, Corbett carried on a one-man war against
poachers with blandishments and threats. Old residents swear
that he knocked down the gun of a poacher as he carried it on
his shoulder parallel to the ground with a well-aimed rifle shot
on the butt. Perhaps it was a prod from the Association that
made Corbett sit down to write as well.

When did Corbett take to writing? The *Hoghunter's An-
nual*, vol. IV, of 1931, published the story of the Pipal Pani
Tiger, now included in Corbett's *Man-Eaters of Kumaon*. The
Annual, devoted to the 'noble art' of pigsticking and the
activities of the tent clubs all over the world, was edited by
Capt. H. Nugent Smith and Capt. J. Scott Cockburn from
Naini Tal and published by the *Times of India* Press in
Bombay. Corbett was not a pigsticker, though he looked after
the assets of the Meerut Tent Club when it wound up at the
beginning of World War II. I have it from Cockburn that
Corbett was not approached to write. It could have been
Ibbotson who brought the story for publication. Ibbotson,
also a pigsticker, certainly competed in 1934 and 1936 for
the Kadir Cup, the Hoghunter's most coveted trophy.

His second dated writing on wildlife was in the *Review
of the Week* of 31 August 1932. The *Review* was published
by the Assistant Superintendent-in-Charge, Government
Branch Press, Naini Tal, and his article, taking up the whole
of the back page, was headed: 'Wild Life in the Village: An
Appeal.'

I am reproducing the article in full for three reasons: first,
it shows the growth of the hunter into a conservationist;
second, doubts have been raised as to Corbett's competence

as a writer; and third, it is the swansong of the wildlife of the foothills. The article reads:

It was a small village of some 16 ploughs differing in no respect from hundreds of similar villages, scattered throughout the length of the tract along the Bhabar. Originally the village had been surrounded by tree jungle intercepted with grass and in this virgin jungle lived all the numerous denizens of the wild. To protect their crops the villagers erected thorn fences round their fields. As an additional safeguard a member of the depressed class was encouraged to settle in the village whose duty it was to watch the crops at night and see they were not damaged by stray cattle and wild animals. Owing to the abundance of game, tigers did not interfere with the village cattle and I cannot remember a single case of cow or bullock having been killed by a tiger. In the course of time, a great change took place not only in the villagers themselves but also in the jungle surrounding the village. Hindus, who formerly looked upon the taking of life as against their religious principles, were now clamouring for gun licenses and were competing with each other in the indiscriminate slaughter of game. As profits from the sale of game increased, field work was neglected and land began to go out of cultivation. Simultaneously, *lantana*, introduced into Haldwani as a pot plant, started to kill out the grass and *basonta* until the village was surrounded with a dense growth of this obnoxious weed. Government now stepped in and at great expense built a pucca wall all round the village. The building of this wall freed the villagers from the necessity of erecting fences and watching their crops and gave them more time to devote to the killing of the game. This *heavy and unrestricted shooting of deer had the inevitable consequence of disturbing the balance in nature with the result that tigers and leopards, that had hitherto lived on game, were now forced to live on the village cattle.* One morning in May of the present year [1932], I arrived in the village and pitched my tent in a little clearing just outside the cultivated land. News of my arrival soon spread through the village and in a short time a dozen men were squatting in front of my tent. One and all had some tale to tell. *A tiger had taken up its quarters in the lantana and in the course of two years had killed 150 head of cattle, and unless it was destroyed the village would have to be abandoned.* While the men were pouring out their tale of woe, I observed a pair of vultures circling low over a narrow stretch of lantana running between the village men and the public road. The two vultures were soon pointed at by others; so picking up a rifle, I set off to investigate. Progress through the lantana was difficult but with the aid of a good hunting knife a way was eventually cut and the remains of a horse killed the previous day found. There were plenty of pug marks round the kill, little of which remained, and it was easy to locate the tiger from his low continuous growling but impossible to see him in the dense cover. Returning to the road, which was only 40 yards round the kill and little used at this time of year, I concealed myself behind a bush in the hope that the tiger would follow me to see if I had left the locality, quite a natural thing for it to do. *Half an hour later the tiger walked out on to the road and gave me an easy shot as he stood facing me.* That evening—after I had skinned the tiger—he was *a very old animal and I took four old bullets and nine pellets of buck-shots out of him*—I called the villagers together and made an appeal to them on behalf of the few remaining deer in the jungle.

On the opposite side of the village from my camp, *irrigation water had been allowed to flow into the jungle. Over this water machans had been built in the trees and in these machans men sat through the heat of the day, and all night long on moonlit nights, and shot down animals that came to drink.*

There was no other water within miles and *if a thirst-maddened animal avoided one machan, it fell a victim to the man in the next.* I told the villagers that *God had given water free for all* and that *it was a shameful thing for men to sit over the water God had provided and shoot His creatures when they came to drink.* To do this was to lower themselves below a corpse-eating hyena, for even he, the lowest of all creation, did not lie in wait to kill defenceless animals while they were drinking. The men listened to me in silence and when I had done, said they had not looked at the matter in this light, and they promised that they would take down the *machans* they had erected and in future would not molest the animals that came to the vicinity of the village to drink. I stayed in the locality several weeks, taking bird and animal pictures, and am glad to say the men kept their promise. I believe that much of the slaughter of deer that is daily taking place throughout the length and breadth of the Bhabar and Tarai would cease if an appeal was made to the better feelings of men. *I do not exaggerate the damage that is being done to our fauna by shooting over water.* Let me give you but one instance. An acquaintance of mine living in a village in the Bhabar adjoining mine, in one hot season, over one small pool of water shot, with a single-barrel muzzle-loading gun, 60 heads of *cheetal* and *sambhar* which he sold in a nearby bazaar at the rate of Rs 5 per *cheetal* and Rs 10 per *sambhar*. It is no exaggeration to say that the *banks of every little stream and every pool of water in the vicinity of Bhabar villages are soaked with the blood of animals that never took toll of a single blade of the villagers' crops.* I assert without fear of contradiction that *for every shot fired on cultivated land from guns provided for crop protection, a hundred shots are fired in the jungle over water.*

Pigs and *neelgai* are the only wild animals that damage the crops in the Bhabar to any extent, and to keep them out of cultivated land Government has expended lakhs of rupees in building pucca walls. *It is asserted that in recent years tigers have increased. With this assertion I do not agree.* It is a fact that *more cattle are being killed every year; this is not due to tigers having increased but due to the balance in nature having been disturbed by the unrestricted slaughter of game,* and also to some extent to tigers having been driven out of their natural haunts where they were seldom or never seen by man, by the activities of the Forest Department. *A country's fauna is a sacred trust, and I appeal to you not to betray your trust.* Shooting over water, shooting over salt licks, natural and artificial, shooting birds in the close season and when roosting at night, encouraging permit-holders to shoot hinds, fencing off large areas of forest and the extermination by the Forest Department of all game within these areas, making unnecessary motor tracks through the forest and shooting down from motor cars, the absence of sanctuaries and the burning of forests by the Forest Department and by villagers at a time when the forests are full of young life are all combining to one end—the extermination of our fauna. If we do not bestir ourselves now, it will be to our discredit that the fauna of our province was exterminated in our generation and under our very eyes, while we looked on and never raised a finger to prevent it.—(Major Corbett).

The article has been reproduced without any change, and the italics are Corbett's own for emphasis. And shall we call him a Jeremiah?

While lecturing boys and girls in Naini Tal's schools in the 1930s and 1940s, little did Corbett realize that the knowledge of the jungle he was imparting to the youngsters would be put to adult use and that he would don an army uniform again one day to instil confidence into young officers of the Allied nations to face the rigours of life in the forest. These were what were later known as the Chindits, under training for the Burma campaign.

Corbett was sixty-four when World War II broke out. Again he offered his services to the army, and again the army would have nothing to do with an old man. Undaunted, the Major in the Indian Army Reserve of Officers found a way to contribute his mite to the war effort. Welfare was close to his heart and he agreed to become vice-president of the District Soldiers' Board that looked after the needs of the families of serving men. This involved a lot of travelling and miscellaneous work like writing letters, tracing missing personnel and rendering help to servicemen's families in distress.

Simultaneously, he started recruitment for the Civil Pioneer Corps. The term lasted from 1940 to 1942. In 1942, the job was interrupted by serious sickness, an attack of tick typhus. Corbett was in hospital for three months. He was released with a warning that he should now take things easy and that the strenuous life he had been leading would be dangerous to his health. But the old warrior made a quick recovery and was soon clamouring for another opportunity. This came in the form of an assignment very close to his heart: would he train troops in junglecraft?

In February 1944 Corbett was commissioned a Lieutenant-Colonel and appointed senior instructor in jungle lore at a centre the army had opened at Chhindwara, in Madhya Pradesh (formerly Central Provinces). Leading the strenuous life of a training camp, he could not keep up the pace and was laid up in eighteen months with a severe attack of malaria. He went back to Kaladhungi in September 1945 and was nursed through sickness by Maggie, who herself was stricken with the same disease. But before the war ended his first book was out and he had plans to write more.

What did he teach in Chhindwara? The Defence Ministry

Historical Section could not produce a thing on this and we
have perforce to go back to *Jungle Lore* to dig up facts about
the instructor's activities. For a month he devoted himself to
a study of the flora and fauna of Burma and then reported
at Chhindwara ready to teach.

The British generals had realized after the rout in Burma
that the Japanese could only be defeated if their jungle war
techniques could be matched with something better. Gen.
Orde Charles Wingate, basing himself on his experience in
Ethiopia, laid down the first principles of jungle war. In this,
the orthodox principles of war are considerably diluted and
detachments living off the country or fed from the air make
deep forays into enemy territory as fighting patrols.

One psychologically inhibiting factor was the city upbringing of the Allied officer class who found themselves completely lost in the jungle. Corbett had to prepare them for
the task ahead and convince them that the jungle was a living
thing, and once the rudiments of junglecraft were acquired
it was more hospitable than the desert which is the city. In
the jungle one 'could live at peace with all wildlife'.[11]

Corbett was in his element now. One morning at Chhindwara he gave his first performance before a draft, which
luckily contained some keen bird-watchers. He demonstrated
his mastery of junglecraft by calling a screaming serpent eagle
low for closer scrutiny by fishing out a reed whistle from his
bush-shirt pocket and blowing at it. That was an imitation
of the cry of a fawn in distress. His only regret was that the
eagle could not be brought closer for a photograph as well.
He used the reed whistle for a signalling system, as it was a
natural sound that would not attract the enemy in the forest.

The main accent was, however, on survival. These lessons
were on direction-finding, identification of edible flowers,
fruits and tubers, the pinpointing of sounds, and training the
eye to a full field of 180 degrees of vision. An applied
junglecraft lesson sought to teach soldiers how to assess the

[11] *Jungle Lore*, p. 154.

human tracks on a jungle path, the number of men in a party, if loaded or unloaded, and if hurrying—there are then more toe marks and fewer heel marks. The apothecary's son also taught about the medicine available in the jungle for wounds, fevers, sore throat and stomach disorders. Further, he gave instructions on how to kill game without a firearm and prepare tea without a metal pot. In an aside in *Jungle Lore*, Corbett sought the forgiveness of those he trained if 'he worked them hard'. It had to be so, for 'time was short'.

10 Writer

FEW AUTHORS take so kindly to their publishers as to mention them in their wills. However, the top executives of Oxford University Press in Bombay, London and New York figure in the Corbett will. The first got a carpet and nine volumes of his illustrated Shakespeare, the second a carpet, and the third a maneater tiger skin. Oxford University Press discovered Corbett the writer and made a major impact on his life and fortunes.

Man-Eaters of Kumaon, the manuscript of which was a substantial rehash of *Jungle Stories*, a book Corbett had written and printed privately in 1935, was submitted to the Bombay branch of OUP in 1943. When the manuscript arrived, R.E. Hawkins (one of the three mentioned in the will and Corbett's editor) soon realized he had a winner, the second great maneater book of the century after the publication of J.H. Patterson's *Man-Eaters of Tsavo* in 1907.

Corbett's idea in submitting the manuscript was philanthropic. He wanted to contribute the proceeds to St Dunstan's for the benefit of a newly opened centre for the war-blinded in India. According to Hailey, Corbett had not the remotest idea of the book's worth. 'I remember how modest was his own estimate of what this contribution might be. He did not realize how enthralling were the stories he had to tell, nor how greatly their interest would be enhanced by his manner of telling them. Yet, as the world was soon to acknowledge, he possessed, in fact, that supreme art of narrative which owes nothing to conscious artistry.'[1]

1

Introduction to *Tree Tops*.

Man-Eaters of Kumaon was dedicated to the 'gallant soldiers, sailors and airmen of the United Nations who during 1939–1945 lost their sight in the service of their country'. The idea of writing *Jungle Stories* came to Corbett at Government House, Naini Tal where, as a narrator of his maneater exploits, he had already acquired quite a reputation at the dinner table. 'Why don't you put it down?' a governor's wife had asked him. And what was the manuscript of *Man-Eaters* like? According to Hawkins, there was very little to be done except resist the temptation to cut out repetitions. Corbett's style was conversational and he had the knack of gradually building up tension. He never kept notes, but with his photographic memory he could relive each moment of an encounter with a maneater.

A letter Corbett wrote to Maggie on 11 April 1930, after killing the Chowgarh tigress, pointed out the necessity of keeping the record straight for 'from scraps of conversation I heard before dinner, the story, although only three hours old, is already distorted, and will be unrecognizable by the time it gets to Naini, per the bearer of this'.[2] While writing the story some eleven years later, he never checked the letter for the facts and the finished story is just the same in all its essentials.

And to silence a host of schoolmasters and typists at Naini Tal, who claimed to have rewritten or corrected the manuscript, Hawkins affirmed that all Corbett's books 'are his unaided work', except for the help he got from Maggie, who also had a good memory. When the book was written, Corbett's exploits were already legendary in Kumaon.

Hawkins also said: 'Corbett inspired confidence and reliance. The understatement which characterizes his writings was characteristic of him too . . . I knew many people who knew him at different periods of his life, and all agree that he was modest and reliable, and a superlative woodsman.'

The manuscript of *Man-Eaters* was submitted in August

[2] Cumberlege's introduction to World's Classics edition of *Man-Eaters of Kumaon* and *The Temple Tiger*.

1943, and the book published in August 1944. In true Corbett style, he found the two biggest in the land to sponsor the book: Lord Linlithgow, whom Corbett had hosted at tiger hunts at Kaladhungi, wrote the foreword, and Sir Maurice Hallett the preface. Linlithgow wrote: 'These stories are the true account of Maj. Corbett's experiences with maneating tigers in the jungles of the United Provinces . . . I can with confidence write of him that no man with whom I have hunted in any continent better understands the signs of the jungle.'

The first chapter to be written was 'Robin'. Corbett probably completed *Man-Eaters* while ill at Agra in 1942. The book was immediately a tremendous success. As a young man of twenty-three, I well remember staying up the whole night to finish it, it was so gripping. Friends who borrowed the book had the same thrilling experience. Sometimes entire families huddled together the whole night, all ears, to hear it read aloud.

The book was reprinted in Britain, Canada and the United States in 1946. By 1955 it had been translated into at least sixteen languages, among them French, German, Italian, Swedish, Norwegian, Dutch, Czech, Spanish, Portuguese, Japanese and Indonesian. Six translations are available in Indian languages. There is a Sinhala edition. The Russians reprinted it as an English text. It is also a talking book for the blind for whom its earnings were intended. Corbett was always delighted to hear of each new translation.

After *Man-Eaters*, his next book was *The Man-Eating Leopard of Rudraprayag*, published in 1948. The writing of this book was interrupted because a maneater (his last) had to be killed. *My India* followed in 1952 'in response to hundreds of letters I have received from America and other people of India'.[3] *Jungle Lore* came in 1953 and the *Temple Tiger* in 1954. The second book is dedicated to the 'victims of the maneating leopard of Rudraprayag', the third to the 'poor of India' and the fourth to Maggie. The fifth and sixth

[3] Letter to J.S. Negi.

books went without a dedication. The last was *Tree Tops*, published posthumously in 1955. That is his only book with an African setting.

While it was launched quietly in Britain, OUP New York marked the publication of *Man-Eaters of Kumaon* with much ballyhoo. The New York book trade was invited to a cocktail party in the ballroom of Hotel Pierre to be greeted by two twelve-month-old tiger cubs specially flown from Florida in a private plane to autograph a copy for the author who 'was unable to get reservations to New York to celebrate the publication of the book'. The quote is from the American *Publishers' Weekly*. The journal also had a photograph of a cub being helped to 'footprint' a copy for the author.

The first full-page advertisements featuring tiger foot-prints appeared in the *New York Times Book Review* and the *New York Herald Tribune Weekly Book Review*. The American Book-of-the-Month Club issued *Man-Eaters of Kumaon* and *The Snake Pit*, by Mary Jane Ward, as a double attraction in April 1946, two books for the price of one. *The Snake Pit* is a novel on the mentally ill.

Henry Z. Walck, then President of Oxford University Press Inc., New York, who had the Thak maneater skin spruced up for a photograph, was the architect of the publicity. He wrote:

I think our publicity campaign for *Man-Eaters of Kumaon* was one of the best we ever launched. Jim Corbett was not unknown in the United States for he had helped train US troops in jungle fighting. The subject was of interest to a great number of people and his writing style was excellent. We were justified in launching an all-out campaign.

We arranged with the New York Zoological Society to make footprints from one of the tigers in the zoo for reproduction and use in the book. Obtaining these footprints added a few gray hairs to John Begg, who was our Art Director and Production Manager, but he did get successful ones.

One of the ink manufacturers was then experimenting with luminous ink printing. We had posters printed using this luminous ink for the tiger's eyes. The posters were furnished to book stores who used them in their windows with good effect. In fact the eyes glowed for a time after the lights were turned off at night. Requests for copies of this poster long after publication tended to keep the interest alive.

Considering the American press reviews, the dramatic publicity was worthwhile. Sterling North, in the *New York Post*, commented: 'The format of the book was rather forbidding and the photographs amateurish. But I wish to go on record as saying that in many years of book reviewing I have seldom been carried away by a factual recital . . . how Corbett could force himself to wade into chin-deep tangles of grass after wounded tigers . . . or track the big cats into jungles no native had dared traverse in five years, not even the enthusiastic sponsors of the book can explain.' The sponsors were a Viceroy and a Governor.

Christopher Morley, in the *Book-of-the-Month Club News*, called it 'a story of murder, of detective skill and courage, also of natural history, of the life of primitive people, of marvellous scenic beauty, and an unconscious revelation of rare human character. . . . The chapter on his half-breed spaniel, Robin, who was an invalid with a bad heart, is one of the most charming tributes in all the peculiar literature on dogs.'

James Hilton, commenting on the biographical material in the book, called it the self-portrait of 'a man in whom an intense kinship with nature has quieted many of the problems that beset the rest of us' and that the portrait was so clear because it was 'largely unconscious'. A lone faultfinder was Edmund Wilson, who said 'even the style in spots is like ruptured Kipling'.

British press reactions were equally warm. J.W. Turner wrote in the *Spectator*: 'Often my heart almost stopped, and I had to lay down the book, it was so exciting. But these are exploits of such quality that they can be read over and over again. And they will be read with an evergrowing respect for the brave and humane man who tells simply and honestly of his misgivings on having once shot a sleeping tiger.'

By the middle of May 1946 there were 536,000 copies of *Man-Eaters* in print. The Americans, having nothing bigger in cats than the mountain lion, were thrilled with the hair-raising exploits of the hunter. Back in Naini Tal, Corbett too felt the impact of the distant limelight. He was swamped with fan mail. To a friend who called at Gurney House one morning in mid-1946, he ruefully showed a pile of letters as he sat at his typewriter banging out replies. A letter from the US offered to send him f.o.b. Bombay a dog answering best to Robin's description. It was a sunny morning and Corbett would have preferred to take a walk.

As an aside, the friend remembered Maggie bringing in a fledgeling fallen from its nest and wondering what was wrong with it as it lay lackadaisically in her cupped palm. 'Over-feeding, I suppose', Corbett said. He lifted the seat cover from his box sofa chair and put it in, continuing the conversation on the problems of limelight with his friend. Soon the mother bird came cheeping in. The lid was raised, the fledge-ling was taken out and the mother and young one disappeared into the garden.

Another visitor to the Corbett house in those days was Christine Griswold, better known as Christine Weston, author of *Indigo*, a novel published in the 1940s. Christine, born at Unnao in UP, had studied at Naini Tal. Though her memories of Corbett, she says, are 'nothing very vivid', she recalls that he was 'very gentle, very quiet, very reserved, never talked much'. And he would never talk about himself. One thing that really struck her was his memory for people and places and his extraordinary knowledge of nature.

When Universal Pictures approached the New York office of OUP for permission to film *Man-Eaters of Kumaon*, Corbett agreed to Monty Shaff and Frank P. Rosenberg produc-ing it because it would give him a chance to show to the readers the 'men and women I have mentioned and the streams, trees, and rocks I have drawn attention to'. Alas, the excitement died down when the Government of India refused permission to shoot the film on location. The end result was a poor film, *Man-Eater of Kumaon*, with a mangled story, the handiwork of four screen writers, Jeanne Bartlett, Lewis

Meltzer, Richard G. Hubler and Alden Nash. Corbett had
liked the first film script. He was bitter not only with the
Government of India for refusing to let the film be shot in
Kumaon, but also with Hollywood. No wonder Corbett did
not like the final version of the film, for the hunter had
become a neurotic American who didn't want to follow up
the tiger he had wounded and who was finally killed by it.
Corbett told Christine Griswold that the best actor in the
film was the tiger.

Corbett called at the Indian High Commission at Nairobi
once and had lunch with the High Commissioner, Apa B.
Pant. The diplomat was not very popular with the Whites
of Kenya. He was in Kenya from 1948 to 1954. Perhaps the
Government of India's decision figured in their luncheon
conversation.

And what did Corbett think of his writing? The Corbett
museum has a blown-up photograph of two handwritten
sentences by him: 'Don't be too critical. A jungli can only tell
his stories in jungle language.' Elsewhere he says: 'For having
lived the greater part of my life in the jungles I have not the
ability to paint word pictures.'[4] What a master of understatement for all the fine prose he produces—the suspense he
builds as a narrative artist, the word pictures he paints of
Himalayan sunsets, and the morning and vesper songs of birds.
And in this he takes his place with other adventurous contemporaries: Peter Fleming, T.E. Lawrence, Spencer Chapman,
J.H. Williams and Thor Heyerdahl. Here was accomplish-
ment truthfully recorded in vibrant prose. Apart from *Tree
Tops*, which was out of print for some years but has once more
been reprinted by Oxford University Press, all of Corbett's
other books have remained in print without a break and been
repeatedly reprinted. They continue to be read avidly by new
generations of readers and conservationists, and are deservedly
treated as classics.

[4] *Man-Eaters of Kumaon*, p. 247.

11 Just Jim

HAVING KNOWN Carpet Sahib, we shall now turn to Jim the friend of the hunter and fisherman. All his books are dotted with the names of collectors appealing to the hunter to rid their districts of maneaters. Then there were governors, viceroys and generals asking for favours. Could he please get them a tiger or two?

It is hard at times to draw the line between friendship and patronage. He fished the Sharada and Ramganga with Hailey. He fixed at least three tiger shoots for Linlithgow and fished the Ramganga with him. When shooting, perhaps with Hailey, at Bindukhera in 1929, a high-velocity rifle fired by a spectator behind him on the howdah burst his eardrum and he had to make a quick, quiet retreat from the camp on the pretext of urgent work. It was confirmed in Naini Tal that the injury was severe, and so he went to Lahore to see Col Dick, an ear specialist, armed with a letter from Hailey. In three months the specialist 'restored my hearing sufficiently for me to associate with my fellowmen without embarrassment, and gave me back the joy of hearing music and the song of birds'.[1]

Hailey, who continued to be a lifelong friend, wrote in the March 1946 issue of the *American Book-of-the-Month Club News* marking the launching of *Man-Eaters*: 'Even in his later years, he retains the spare form, the untiring muscles and insensibility to hardship or hunger which long days and nights in the jungles and on the hills demand. And he has

[1] *The Temple Tiger*, p. 180.

rare gifts of eye and hand. To those who use the 12 bore gun for small game, there is something uncanny in his performance with his light 28 bore; his handling of the rifle for big game recalls some of the storied feats of the Wild West gunmen; and how often have I not looked with envy on his mastery over the fighting fish of the Kumaon rivers.'

The ear accident in 1929 nearly spelt disaster, for one of Corbett's worst hunts, of the Talla Des maneater, followed it. With an abscess in the ear and a swollen face, he trailed the wounded tigress for days and part of a night. He was warned after the accident not to fire a heavy rifle. A ·275 rifle bought in Calcutta then became his favourite. It was easy to carry and ideal for hill shooting, though not the best for a tiger hunt.

With all the leisure available to Corbett with the acquisition of the Naini Tal business and his return to town after the railway period in 1919, it was natural for sportsmen to seek him out. Even in his railway days he had proved himself a top hunter by killing at least three maneaters.

An early patron was Percy Wyndham, 'who knew more about tigers than any other man in India'. He fished and hunted with him in the Bhabar and the Tarai, and part of the time chased a bandit named Sultana. Wyndham, a colourful Commissioner of Kumaon, had a lot in common with Corbett. Both were bachelors with a passion for the tiger and devoted all their spare time to blood sports. Both wore shorts as their nether garment and, indifferently dressed, avoided women.

Wyndham considered meeting policemen and Brahmins a bad omen and was known to have abandoned a shoot, for, as he started out on an elephant from the dak bungalow, these were the two callers on the Commissioner Sahib. He was fluent in the eastern dialect of UP, which he had acquired in Mirzapur district where he had worked for eighteen years, devoting more than his leisure to tiger hunting with the assistance of his twenty Kole and Bhunya trackers. He brought four of them to Kumaon on his transfer. When the bandobast was made in the Commissioner Sahib's camp, liquor for the trackers was the first concern. He always kept his trackers happy. He was a dyed-in-the-wool bureaucrat who successfully ruled Kumaon by dividing the two major Hindu communities, the Brahmins and Kshatriyas. Some said he sold tiger skins. But he combined a heart of gold with a dour facade. Wyndham Falls in Mirzapur district commemorate his memory in eastern UP.

Wyndham was in Mirzapur as early as 1900. *The Hoghunter's Annual*, Vol. IX, quotes him as telling H. Branford, founder of the Mirzapur Tent Club: 'Produce the cover near water and the pig will come.' Like Corbett, he was not a pigsticker.

Corbett's next patron was A.W. Ibbotson, also of the ICS. As Deputy Commissioner of Garhwal he looked after the arrangements while Corbett was hunting the leopard of Rudraprayag. Ibbotson, a Wrangler and an officer in the Indian Army Reserve of Officers (having fought in World War I), took pride in calling himself one of the 'Seven Devils of the Indian Civil Service'. He too was a divide-and-rule empire builder on the lines of Wyndham. He was a great horseman, shoed his horses himself, could cut his own hair using two mirrors, and made rope as a hobby. Ibbotson, who later became 'Ibby' to Corbett, kept up this hunting and fishing friendship all his life.

As Commissioner of Kumaon, he fished the Sharada with Corbett and accompanied him on the Thak and Chuka maneater hunts. A rare compliment Corbett paid him was: 'Except when accompanied by Ibbotson, I have made it a hard-and-fast rule to go alone when hunting maneaters, for if one's companion is unarmed it is difficult to protect him, and if he is armed it is even more difficult to protect oneself.'[2] Then again, in another context, he said: 'Of all the men I have been on shikar with Ibbotson is by far and away the best, for not only has he the heart of a lion, but he thinks of everything, and with it all is the most unselfish man that carries the gun.'[3]

[2] *Man-Eaters of Kumaon*, p. 36.
[3] Ibid., p. 207.

Wyndham retired in the late 1920s and, as already noted, left for Tanganyika, where he lived half the year on his Kikafu farm growing coffee and maize. Ibbotson retired to Kenya and lived in Nairobi for a time. After Kenya got its independence, Mrs Ibbotson left Kenya and settled in South Africa.

Among the close friends Corbett made in the Forest Service was G.M. Hopkins (Geoff), who as a stripling met him in 1921 on his first posting in the Ramnagar Forest Division. Kaladhungi comes under it. When Hopkins first called on the Corbetts the family included the mother, stepsister Mary Doyle and Maggie. Hopkins was for three years in Ramnagar on his first stint and often dropped in on the Corbetts at Kaladhungi on his winter tours and at Naini Tal in the rains. He was posted elsewhere in 1924, but returned as Divisional Forest Officer in 1933 and remained there till 1942, visiting Corbett and Maggie at Kaladhungi every now and again. The mother and the stepsister were dead by then.

A warm relationship was established between the two when Corbett decided to initiate the young forest officer into the realm of sport shooting and fishing in the nearby Baur river. Hopkins admired him a great deal and as a mentor. 'He was simple, a teetotaller but a great smoker of cigarettes. Friendly to all, he was most unassuming', Hopkins wrote, recollecting the days he spent with him. He kept in touch with him till Corbett died. Hopkins felt it was silly of him to leave India, for 'he was well known, loved and much respected all over that part of UP, chiefly the Kumaon civil division. He was very good to all the local villagers and looked after them like a father, while his sister was very popular with the womenfolk.'

Geoff Hopkins, who was kind enough to write long letters to this biographer, has been mentioned at least three times in *Jungle Lore*—as part of Wyndham's unsuccessful attempts to catch a python for Lucknow Zoo, the preparations for the first Linlithgow shoot, and a chance meeting with Corbett on the bank of the Baur river with Maggie. At the last meeting, getting down from Geoff's elephant, Corbett ran into a tiger feeding on a chital in high grass. Geoff was looking for game to feed some guests. Giving an intimate account of life in Kaladhungi after Corbett's return from the railways and World War I, Hopkins wrote:

In the period 1921–24, my wife and I frequently visited the Corbetts, usually at tea time. Old Mrs Corbett could not get about much and Mary used to stay at home to look after her, while Maggie and Jim came to tea with us at the forest bungalow—a few hundred yards away. Their bungalow was really a pretty indifferent sort of place in those days—of course they lived there for only a few months in the cold weather.

. . . At that time only the women slept in the bungalow. Jim had a very small tent on a concrete slab in the garden as a bedroom. Later on, after 1924, Jim built another room, alongside but detached from the bungalow, which he used. . . . Most of our forest bungalows were superior to and more comfortable than the Corbett place.

They lived very simply indeed, did most if not all their cooking and had only one or two servants as compared with the horde of servants and camp followers it was the British official's custom to maintain. The only beverage was tea, masses of it at any odd time. I do not think they ever had even coffee in those days, and certainly no alcohol. I think they had to live very simply as they could not afford to do otherwise, even if they had wanted to, which they probably didn't. I think they regarded the annual stay at Kaladhungi as 'just camping out'. Their bungalow at Naini Tal was very different, well and fully furnished.

At that time there was only a bridle path on the direct route to Naini Tal, about 15 miles in length. Jim and Maggie used to walk up and down while Mrs Corbett and Miss Doyle went in dandies. When the latter two had died, Maggie used to have a dandie but Jim always walked. I don't remember him ever riding a pony. He was a terrific walker and more than once quite exhausted me.

A little about Maggie—she worshipped her brother but, in a quiet way, had a great deal of influence on him and got her own way when she wanted to. Her stepsister, Mary, dominated her while she was alive, but after that Maggie ran the establishment. She was very good to the local villagers and would always help them in difficulties . . . When I was there, she bought the dhobi a new pony, or maybe it was a donkey, when his was killed by a leopard. The animal carried the laundry to the dhobi ghat and back.

In another context, he wrote:

Without appearing to be snobbish, I must try to explain the social setup in those days, in the twenties let's say. There were grades in the services to start with, the ICS thinking themselves superior to the Police, PWD and Forest Services—that is the so-called Superior Services, Imperial or All-India. Then there was the provincial services grade, lower down, non-officials ('I'll leave out the 'box-wallahs' as there were practically no business people in and about Naini Tal then) and then the 'country-born'. Anglo-Indians were another grade. The various grades hardly met socially. Corbett was not a member of the club [Naini Tal Yacht Club] for very many years and even when he was he hardly ever used it as he wasn't used to the elevated society. Similarly, Maggie would (until much later) feel awkward and out of place if entertained, to tea for example, by some official memsahib. I'm afraid we, the British, were terrible snobs. I suppose that I myself started that way but soon got out of it.

Maggie was a very kind and simple woman. I'm sure she regretted having to leave India. She was old-fashioned—Victorian one might say. She used to come out with my wife and me on local shoots and often accompanied Jim on his evening outings. She was very proud and happy to bask in Jim's reflected glory when he had become famous, and why not? She and my then wife (who is now dead and I remarried) corresponded pretty regularly while she was in Kenya and until Maggie died. . . . One of Maggie's particular interests was in birds. She was always feeding the birds and watching them in their Kaladhungi and Naini Tal gardens.

In those days, Hopkins felt, Corbett's interests were limited to hunting, fishing and photography. Linlithgow's two shoots were held in his division, one at Kaladhungi and the other at Ramnagar. A Governor's shoot (Hallett's) was also held in his division near Kaladhungi.

A friend of Maggie that I met in 1972 was Miss W. Kenny of Lady Hardinge Homes, Simla. She was in Naini Tal between 1940 and 1964 as secretary of the local YWCA.

Maggie was its president for a time. Apart from her activities connected with hospital welfare, Maggie and Miss Kenny looked after the local coolies (the men who pushed the rickshaws and carried the loads). In one particular winter, they distributed 600 blankets to them. Miss Kenny well remembered that they all tried to get Corbett interested in welfare work, but he never agreed to get mixed up in it. She thought that basically he was a 'man's man, also shy like the animals he loved'.

About Corbett's books, Miss Kenny said Naini Tal wags insisted that there was considerable help from Ibbotson when Jim wrote his first book. Town gossip also had it that Mrs Ibbotson was sore that the Corbett publishers had been mentioned in the will and 'he had not the grace to recompense the Ibbotsons for the help given'. Also, one of the reasons why Corbett decided to go to Kenya was that he wanted to be near Ibbotson, his literary mentor.

Miss Kenny was proud of the fact that she was the first to break the news of the renaming of a national park after Corbett to Maggie. Maggie wrote to G.B. Pant thanking him. Maggie, she said, was 'just ordinary and could not make a mark anywhere'. The Corbetts were not social and did little or no entertaining. Maggie, she said, liked rugs and bought a lot when leaving for Kenya.

Among Corbett's close Indian friends, Rai Bahadur Jai Lal Sah was Corbett's neighbour at Choti Haldwani. His family, which got a land grant at Kaladhungi for its loyalty to the Crown during the Uprising of 1857, later bought the Murray Hotel estate opposite Corbett's house. Sah and Corbett sat on the Naini Tal Municipal Board together and were honorary magistrates part of the time. From Kenya, Corbett often turned to him for help to straighten out matters connected with his estate. Mathura Datt Pande, also a city father, was Corbett's lawyer. The Pande family has a double-nut Seychelles coconut shell which Corbett brought from Africa. Jagat Singh Negi, former toll superintendent of the Naini Tal Municipal Board, who lived in one of the outhouses of Gurney House, had links with the family dating back to the heyday of Matthews and Company. He later ran errands for Corbett and Maggie. He worshipped Corbett, so did his pretty wife.

As a person with some business interests, Corbett courted all the big Sahs of the town, a colourful community of Naini Tal businessmen in their own right, who competed with each other for favours from the Raj and the best nautch girls of the province. These were also his associates in buying and selling property.

He was familiar with all the Forest Department people, kindred spirits who lived in the wilds and loved it. A common Corbett trait was leaving Rs 2 for the benevolent fund of low-paid Forest Department employees whenever he occupied a forest rest-house. The traveller stayed in them free in those days on a hard-to-get permit. The fund was started by F. Canning, Chief Conservator of Forests, UP, to help the families of forest guards who had died in harness. Every forest guard had to subscribe a day's salary a year to the fund. I saw a Corbett entry in the visitors' register maintained at the rest-house at Vinayak on the Naini Tal-Kunj Kharak road. Perhaps Corbett was there for the chukors of Khalar, a village near by, or the koklas pheasant, whose crowing at false dawn is one of the cherished memories of this biographer. Incidentally, this rest-house had a massive collection of Jack London's works, perhaps not one title missing. Visitors were encouraged to donate books to rest-houses.

12 Retreat to Africa

WHEN INDIA became free on 15 August 1947, the serving Britons left first, and then the well-to-do Domiciled ones and the Anglo-Indians. All the resident Whites and near-Whites felt forsaken. The memories of the 1942 Quit India movement were still fresh—a few incidents with racial undertones had been magnified beyond all proportion—and it was the talk that once the British left White women would be molested, the men killed and households ransacked in a wave of terror.

The Corbetts also nursed a family trauma, having lost two of their menfolk in 1857, one from the father's side and the other from the mother's. The poor Whites of Naini Tal turned to Corbett for advice because of his long association with the town. 'Why do you want to leave?' he would say. 'This is your own country.' But why then did he finally leave?

Geoff Hopkins ventured an answer. His impression was that Corbett was 'overwhelmed by his British friends in the ICS, who thought or perhaps even hoped—though that might be too cynical—that India would disintegrate as soon as they left in 1947'. Hopkins himself was an Indophile who, unlike others, stuck to his post in the Indian Forest Service till he retired in 1955, leaving for Britain only after that. His father had been in the ICS.

Corbett had not relished the transfer of power. A villager said that, when questioned about his intentions, Corbett would enigmatically say: 'Your independence has come, who cares for us now?' Then in a weaker moment he confided in an aside: 'See, all our people are leaving, there would be no one left to bury us if we stay here.' Here is Maggie's account:

After independence came in India and our British friends were leaving, we began to realize that it would be very difficult for us to remain, especially as when the time came for one of us to be taken, the contemplation of the other having to live on alone in Gurney House, our home for nearly all the years of our lives and so full of memories, could not be faced.

We, therefore, decided very reluctantly to leave. Our choice of destination fell on Kenya, the reason being that Jim knew the country, and we felt the conditions of life there would be much like those we had been used to in India. Jim had a very serious illness the last year we were in India. We had been on a fishing trip to the Kosi and Ramganga—two very big rivers in Kumaon—and while there Jim was suddenly taken ill with a very high temperature and had to be taken to the Ramsay Hospital, where he was found to be suffering from both benign and malignant malaria. After a day or two in hospital, he also developed pneumonia and was so ill that the doctors despaired of his life. However, with very careful and efficient nursing he gradually improved and was able to leave hospital in about a month.[1]

Corbett now quietly started looking for a buyer for Gurney House. Maggie sold it—furniture and all—on 21 November 1947 to Mrs Kalawati Verma, wife of a friend of Corbett, for Rs 50,000. After the sale deed had been signed, Corbett told Mrs Verma: 'I hope you will be as happy in the house as we have been.' He also significantly pointed out that nobody had ever died in the house. Then he fished out a bunch of letters from his pocket. These were higher offers for the house from others. 'Here is a chance for you to make some money', he said. 'But why didn't you?' Mrs Verma asked. 'Well, you know we had agreed to sell it for Rs 50,000, didn't we?' Maggie's last instructions to Mrs Verma were about the piano: 'It has never been tuned, for it was never removed from where it is.' It is still there.

The Kaladhungi house was also offered to Mrs Verma and

[1] Ruby Beyts' notes.

several other friends, but nobody showed much enthusiasm for a village property, and a power of attorney was left with Corbett's lawyer to dispose it of when a buyer came. Corbett was in a hurry. This house, which is now the Corbett museum, was given away to a friend for a paltry Rs 2,000. The friend made some profit when he sold it to the Forest Department of UP to start the museum.

One likes to think that by selling his properties to friends Corbett was keeping a lane open for a possible return. Though he freed his tenants after he left—that too took quite some time—he maintained legal rights of a sort over the Kaladhungi estate by remitting annually the land revenue of Rs 910 to the government right up to his death. After that, Maggie kept up the payment till she too died. Corbett once offered to buy the Kaladhungi house back from its new owner to give his former tenants a panchayat ghar (community centre). He was also in no hurry to wind up his account at his bank in Naini Tal and maintained it till his death. This was a joint account with Maggie.

The Corbetts left Naini Tal on 30 November 1947. 'The morning we were due to leave, we looked across the waters of the lake, which was indescribably beautiful in the early morning light. Our servants did not help make our departure any easier as they stood with tears trickling down their cheeks as we moved down the hill from the house we knew we should never see again. Accommodation in Bombay at that time was very difficult to find as so many Britons were leaving, and all hotels were fully booked. We were, however, very fortunate in having a friend who put us in his beautiful flat overlooking the sea, while we waited for our ship to sail.'[2]

They went via Lucknow to Bombay. The shorter route would have been via Agra. Perhaps Corbett went there for an easier train connection or to say goodbye to his friends, or to visit the grave of the widow of his benefactor, Mary Matthews. A letter he wrote to Jagat Singh in longhand from

[2] Ruby Beyts' notes.

the *SS Aronda* on 11 December 1947 is a nostalgic one from a rocking boat: 'Our regret at leaving our old house is very great and the further we get from India, the worse we feel at leaving our good and faithful friends.'[3] The ship was due in Mombasa on 14 December but was a day late. Some thirty-one packages, including his hunting trophies, had been dispatched earlier by train to Bombay, but only twenty-one had arrived by the time he sailed. Corbett took this stoically as an old railway hand with the comment: 'Considering the congestion on the railways, we are lucky in getting 21 of the 31 packages.'

On the platform of Lucknow railway station, they left their faithful servant, Ram Singh, as they boarded the Bombay train. The last bit of the letter to Jagat Singh is of infinite tenderness for the old faithful: 'I hope Ram Singh got back to Naini safely. We feel terribly sad leaving him crying on the Lucknow platform. If he is at Naini, tell him I am instructing the bank to pay him Rs 10 per month as long as he looks after the house at Kaladhungi. If he is not in Naini, please write to him in Kaladhungi to this effect.' Apart from the money, Ram Singh was given land opposite the house in Kaladhungi as an extra inducement to stay on. He left Kaladhungi when the Corbett house was sold. With nothing to keep him tied down now to Kaladhungi, he sold his land for a small sum and made for the high hills of Garhwal and his village. Ram Singh continued to get money from Corbett till his death.

For Maggie, who was seventy-two, the sea journey to Mombasa was a new experience. Though a bad sailor, Corbett was a veteran of more than a dozen crossings. He had several reasons for deciding on Kenya. It was a colony where White supremacy was acknowledged. The climate of the White Highlands was equable. It had a rich wildlife and he could indulge in his favourite pastime of animal photography. Also in Kenya were his two closest relations: a niece, Dorothy

[3] Courtesy Corbett museum.

Lincoln-Gordon, in Maragua Fort Hall, and a nephew, Lieut.-Gen. Thomas William Corbett, in Mweiga. The nephew was Chief of General Staff in the Middle East when he retired in 1943. Some of his friends lived on the African continent or were buried there. A brother hunter, Lieut.-Col C.H. Stockley (*Stalking in the Himalayas and Northern India*), was in Tanzania and F.W. Champion (*With a Camera in Tiger-Land* and *The Jungle in Sunlight and Shadow*) was also there organizing the Forest Service.

In true Kenya tradition Corbett checked in at the Outspan Hotel at Nyeri, in the White Highlands, after staying for some time near Nairobi with a friend, perhaps Ibbotson. To be part of history, he occupied the Baden-Powell cottage at the hotel which continued to be the Corbett home till Jim's death. Nyeri is the heart of Kikuyuland. South of it were the native preserves where no White had the right to settle.

We lived very happily in this charming cottage and gradually made the garden into a small bird sanctuary. Some of the birds became so tame as to feed out of our hands. Jim counted 26 varieties of birds, attracted not only by the food we gave them, but also by a lovely little pond at the foot of the verandah steps in which they could bathe. We had several kinds of weavers, besides robins, thrushes, glossy starlings and white eyes, these last being the most responsive of all, coming to the call of a whistle. The tiny cardinal waxbills were perhaps the most confiding of all, picking up at our feet the crumbs dropped by other birds.

It was here in this peaceful spot within sight of Mt Kenya that Jim wrote all his books with the exception of *Man-Eaters of Kumaon*, and a small book, *Jungle Stories*, of which he had had only 100 copies printed by a small printing press in Naini Tal to give to friends.[4]

Corbett often ventured into the Aberdare mountain range overlooking the town to photograph wildlife or to guide the clients of his safari company, called Safariland, started in 1948. He was a director of the company. Sometimes he drove

[4] Ruby Beyts' notes.

out to visit the farm at Mweiga which he shared with two others. He became a partner towards the end of 1947.

Afternoon tea was in the garden, where over the years he managed to tame hordes of birds which flocked to the foster father for beakfuls of cake and sandwich. The conference of the birds was quite an event in the town. Some afternoons, while the Corbetts were away, the servants had orders to lay the covers for the birds. Maggie kept this up till the end. It was in the Kaladhungi tradition where the Corbetts kept a bird table. Baden-Powell too had fed birds.

The brother and sister lived in comfort thanks to the royalties now coming in from his first book. They visited England in 1951 and 1953. Maggie had an operation for a cataract on the second visit. She visited England again after Jim's death.

Corbett wrote often to his friends in Naini Tal. A letter dated 5 June 1950 to Jai Lal Sah, now in the possession of a grandson of Sah, shows concern over his health. Sah was suffering from beriberi. It says:

You have led a very active life and have kept wonderfully well all the years. I have known you, and now that you are not as young as you were when we both sat on the municipal board and served as anari[5] [honorary] magistrates, you should be kind to your body and take a little care of yourself. For you and I, and Hira Lal, are all that are left now of the old Kumaonis. Those were happy days for all of us and it is nice to think now that though we differed occasionally on municipal matters, we remained good friends, and as good friends we will meet again on the other side of the river where we will find Krishna Sah, Kundan Lal, Kishori Lal, Ram Singh, Mathura Datt and many others who have gone before us but whom we still remember as good and valued friends.

The rest of the letter deals with some financial arrangements made for a wall he had asked a contractor to build for Nar Singh, his tenant at Choti Haldwani, and the payment twice over of the village revenue to the government that year, by him and his bank at Naini Tal.

[5] *Anari* means raw in Hindustani.

According to Ruby Beyts, 'Maggie had a nasty accident in 1950. She fell off a chair while adjusting a picture on a wall in their cottage, and broke her hip. She was taken to the little hospital in Nyeri where she spent many weeks. Jim visited her daily, and helped considerably towards her recovery by his constant encouragement and determination that she would soon be well again. Although she walked with a stick for some weeks after she left hospital, due to her own courage and Jim's help she was eventually able to walk unaided—no mean achievement for a young lady in her seventies!'

At the start of this book we noted Corbett's greatest triumph in Africa—a visit with Princess Elizabeth (on her last day as Princess) and her husband, the Duke of Edinburgh, to the famous wilderness hotel called Tree Tops. An account of this forms Corbett's last book, *Tree Tops*, which he completed thirteen days before his death.

It was a moving experience for the old loyalist. On 5 February 1952, as he finished shaving, he got a message that the Princess would be pleased to have him with her on Tree Tops. 'It was a breath-taking telephone message.' Corbett shaved again, rushed for a road pass and drove in his Citroen to the edge of the polo ground, where he had spent the previous day with Maggie at a bridge over a ravine, looking for Mau Mau terrorists who might have designs on the life of the Princess or her husband, who was playing polo there. When his absence from the polo ground was commented on, Corbett had a ready explanation: 'Neither my sister Maggie nor I feel happy in a crowd.'[6]

Perhaps again concerned about the safety of the royal guests, Corbett drove up another track from the polo ground on this special day; he dismissed the driver, and walked up the hill to Tree Tops. The morning was sunny and the lake and the saltlick serene, with a meditating heron and a family of dabchicks skimming over the water in a gorgeous setting of blooming Cape chestnuts. But a herd of forty-seven

[6] *Tree Tops*, p. 5.

elephants that moved into the saltlick gave the hunter some anxious moments, for the lord of the herd was fighting two of his rivals for his harem. As the time for the royal party's arrival approached, there was renewed fighting, trumpeting and screaming. Corbett saw the party arrive. He quickly descended from the platform and escorted the Princess up the ladder ten yards away from the elephants. He carried the Princess' handbag and cine camera.

Royalty baiters, Malcolm Muggeridge for one, would I am sure squirm if they were to read *Tree Tops*. It seemed nature itself had made an extra effort to present on a platter to the visitors the best of African wildlife. And from Corbett's account it was a royal salute. Within minutes, the Princess was busy whirring her camera filming a daring baboon on the old ficus whose branches had held Tree Tops Hotel for twenty-five years. There were elephants milling around the saltlick, also warthogs and rhinos. Even a killing seemed to have been enacted for the Princess when a waterbuck gored another to death in the lake.

As the Princess and the Duke did not smoke, Corbett left the group of six on the balcony out of politeness and slunk to a corner to light his pipe, but the Duke followed him and they discussed the Abominable Snowman. They both knew Eric Shipton the mountaineer. The old hunter was honoured that night with a seat between the two at dinner. After dinner, as others slept he quietly settled down for the night at the top of the ladder to guard the guests again. And there was a need for it because there had been cases of arson around Nyeri and that very year, after the royal visit, Mau Mau warriors burnt down in an act of showmanship the Nyeri Polo Club, where the Duke had played, and Tree Tops Hotel, where royalty had spent a night. Tree Tops was later rebuilt.

The old loyalist closed the book—less than thirty pages of it—with near melodrama. He wrote for the benefit of posterity in the logbook of Tree Tops: 'For the first time in the history of the world a young girl climbed into a tree one day a Princess, and after having what she described as her most thrilling experience she climbed down from the tree the next day a Queen—Gold bless her.'[7]

And reporting on the night, he wrote to Cumberlege: 'I, your humble friend, was honoured by being asked to stay with her [the Princess] and her husband for the 20 hours they spent in the tree. When I helped her into the tree she was a Princess, and when I helped her down she was a Queen.'[8]

The night the Princess spent in Tree Tops her father King George VI died. The news was not broken to her till she had reached the royal lodge at Sagana, where she was staying.

Though the Mau Mau emergency had not been declared yet, 1953 was the year of the worst terror in the White Highlands, particularly around Nyeri. The Corbetts were reasonably safe in their hotel when compared with those Whites on outlying farms. Whites on such farms had elaborate instructions from the Police Commissioner for their safety. For a Mau Mau oath was: 'If I am asked to bring in the head of a European, I must do so.'

Settlers were asked to 'keep a weapon loaded and ready at hand for immediate use, to send all the Kikuyu staff out of the house before dusk, to cover the windows with burglar-proof bars, to avoid leaving the house after dark, to keep one room in the house as a strongroom with iron rations, to illuminate the exterior of the house at night and to sit where one could not be attacked unawares from behind.'

The eleventh and unwritten commandment—thou shalt prod the space under thy bed with a stick before retiring for the night—saved Maggie's life. In the Outspan Hotel one night she ferreted out a Kikuyu hiding under her bed. Any other person under the circumstances would have panicked or shouted for help, but not Maggie Corbett. Holding the stick, she quietly asked him what he wanted. 'Money', he

[7] *Tree Tops*, p. 29.
[8] Cumberlege's introduction to World's Classics edition of *Man-Eaters of Kumaon* and *The Temple Tiger*.

said. 'That's not the way to ask for it. You must get out', she said. She showed him the door and followed him out into the garden, perhaps to close the gate on him. As he was being led out, the Kikuyu knocked the frail little woman down. Hearing the commotion, the guard dogs barked and several lights went up in the hotel. But the man escaped.

According to another version, Maggie was with the burglar for more than an hour praying with him and trying to convince him of the evil of his ways before he escaped into the garden. Also, having no money in the cottage, she offered to go to the hotel office to cash a cheque. Although greatly unnerved by the incident, Maggie refused to leave the cottage and seek the greater safety of the main hotel building.

Corbett had a premonition of what was coming. In a letter in 1950 he wrote to Jai Lal Sah (partly reproduced earlier): 'There are about 120,000 Indians in Kenya and I am sure they are the richest and happiest Indians in any part of the world. Their day and night prayer is that agitators will not come here to set the government against them, as was done with the Indians in South Africa.'

Kenya provided him with excellent opportunities for animal photography. Tree Tops was near by, and when the long rains came elephants descended from the higher reaches of the Aberdare Mountains to within three miles of Nyeri. Corbett shot a long film (also screened at Amen House) of one particular herd till it was destroyed in the interests of public safety. The Kenya Government honoured the hunter by making him an honorary game warden.

The Corbetts had a friend in Ruth Eaden, a big woman living alone and managing a farm on the slopes of Mt Kenya at Naro Moru. A Corbett fan, she had a copy of *Man-Eaters of Kumaon* inscribed by the author: 'I greet you as a friend, for all who read my books are my friends.'[9] A guinea fowl feather was kept in the same book, a souvenir Corbett gave her two months before his death after a trip to Samburu

[9] R.K. Raju in the Sunday *Statesman*, 30 November 1969.

Game Park. She also had Corbett's safari tea cup. Corbett was a great tea swiller. Another frequent visitor to the Corbetts was John Savary, an artist famous for his Kikuyu etchings. But

Jim never kept well in Nyeri. The pneumonia had left him with adhesions in his lungs which made breathing difficult, more particularly owing to the lack of oxygen in the air and the volcanic dust which one breathed constantly, especially during the dry season. Jim was in hospital two or three times with bronchitis, and after each attack his breathing became more difficult. I used sometimes to feel that we should not continue to live in Nyeri, but Jim would say: 'One has to live somewhere.' He gradually lost ground and grew very weak. His thoughts to the last were always for others, and the last words he spoke to me were: 'Always be brave, and try and make the world a happier place for others to live in.'[10]

Two days before his death he told a young visitor: 'Live every day as if it were your last.'

On 19 April 1955 Corbett was removed to hospital after a severe heart attack. He was in considerable pain and died the same day. He is buried in the cemetery of St Peter's Anglican Church at Nyeri where Baden-Powell, that other great tracker, was laid to rest in 1941. Corbett's grave is the only one with an epitaph. In the distance towers the snowy peak of Mt Kenya. Jim and Maggie had both expressed a desire in their wills that they be cremated 'if practicable'. Jim was not cremated, but Maggie, who died on 26 December 1963, was. Her ashes were interred beside her brother's grave. A naturalist, and an ascetic at that, would have preferred not to misappropriate a bit of God's good earth for himself.

There is no mention of a funeral service for Corbett in the records of the church register, but there is an entry for Maggie: 'Jan. 3, 1964, 11 a.m.: Memorial service for Miss M. Corbett and interment of ashes.'

The headstone of the Corbett grave is inscribed thus:

[10] Ruby Beyts' notes.

IN FOND REMEMBRANCE
OF
EDWARD JAMES (JIM) CORBETT
BORN IN NAINI TAL, INDIA
25TH JULY, 1875
DIED IN NYERI
19TH APRIL, 1955

UNTIL THE DAY BREAK, AND
THE SHADOWS FLEE AWAY

HIS SISTER MAGGIE
26-12-1963

The handsome headstone is a square of marble with a single flower carved on the lefthand corner. The epitaph, 'Until the day break . . . ', comes from his mother's grave in the Sukha Tal cemetery at Naini Tal where she was buried next to his father. The slab on the father's grave, of red sandstone, has a solitary rose, but the inscription is obliterated with age. Even the name cannot be deciphered unless one is familiar with it and looks from an angle.[11] This graveyard became crowded with the landslide deaths of 1880 and Archibald and Eugene Mary Doyle are buried in another cemetery of the town. Mary Jane Corbett, the mother, born on 12 March 1837, died on 26 May 1924 at Naini Tal.

After Corbett's death Maggie wrote to Jagat Singh from London:

Life seems very empty without the Sahib, but he told me I must be brave and cheerful and help to make the world a happier place for other people to live in. His thoughts were always for other people, never for himself. He was busy with his writing up to the last and was in hospital for only one day, but he suffered greatly on that day with his heart, for the pain was very intense; but he

---

[11] The slab has since been changed.

bore it bravely and never murmured. I feel he did so much good in the world both by his example and his books.[12]

On 15 March 1957 Maggie sent some money to Jagat Singh for 'distribution to the poor'. Jagat Singh himself got Rs 1,000 as a legacy and Rs 1,500 as travelling expenses for the distribution of the money to temples and other institutions in the area where Corbett had hunted. Maggie, a practical woman, insisted on 'proper receipts for all the payments made'. Each former tenant of Corbett at Kaladhungi got Rs 50 as part of the largesse. This was in the Hindu tradition of giving alms after death, a suggestion Corbett himself made. Maggie was fair to all the communities at Kaladhungi, the mosque getting Rs 500 and the Hindu temple the same amount. The Rudraprayag temple received Rs 1,000, and so did the one at Almora. The Methodist pastors of Kaladhungi and Naini Tal were given Rs 200 and Rs 500 respectively for their personal use. The letter closes 'with best salaams to you all'.

Albert Einstein died on 18 April 1955 at Princeton, New Jersey, and Corbett the next day at Nyeri, Kenya. Though Einstein hit the front page of Indian papers the next day, Corbett's death was unaccountably reported forty-eight hours late. They both were unpretentious wizards, one of mathematics and physics and the other of junglecraft. They both spent a lifetime studying the laws of nature in their own light.

Alas, even after that there were just bare reports in the Indian press on the hunter's death. A leading Bombay daily, which ventured an obituary, called Corbett a former 'district officer'. The Naini Tal Municipal Board adopted a resolution on 30 April 'recording its profound sorrow at the death of Mr Jim Corbett at his new home' and its gratitude for the 'invaluable services the deceased rendered to Kumaon and particularly this town'. An amendment made in the resolution was that the 'Union and the state governments be requested to create a wildlife sanctuary to commemorate the memory

[12] Courtesy Corbett museum.

of Kumaon's greatest sportsman and friend.' Oddly enough,
it did not mention the fact that the hunter was once a member
of the Board.

The best tribute to Corbett I have read was in the London
Times of 4 May 1955 from an unsigned 'friend' of Corbett,
who has later been identified as John Hope, the son of Lord
Linlithgow:

May I try on behalf of some who knew him well, to add a few
personal notes, to your most worthy obituary notice on Jim Corbett? [This appeared on 22 April]. He was a great man. Not only
was he a great genius in the ways of the jungle, as most of them
who have read his books can tell, but he also had in him the depth
and the gentleness that go with the best sort of greatness. With it
went, too, the quietest and softest of voices which was a joy to
listen to whether it was telling you a story about a tiger in the past
or instructing you on how to tackle one in a few minutes' time.
His sense of duty and unselfishness was paramount alike to his
country in war as to the villagers of his Kumaon hills in peace—how
these adored him and how they must be grieving at his passing!

Just before the war, Jim gave me a copy of his original *Jungle
Stories* and on the flyleaf he wrote the words: 'To remind you of
the jungles in which you and I have spent many happy days
together.' Those days are to me, as were similar days to my family,
as happy as any I will ever know. Their essence is as fresh and
compelling as if it had been of yesterday. The earth heavy with
dew in the early morning, turning so soon to dry dust under the
risen sun; the swish of the grass as the elephants ambled slowly
through it; the scarlet of the samal tree blossoms and the gleam of
the Flame of the Forest; the beauty of the birds around you; that
fugitive glimpse of the striped back sliding noiselessly away before
you; then the peaceful evening in Jim's company as you sat in the
night air free from the smell of the paraffin lamps in the tent.

All this and much more made magic by the presence of this
man, comes welling up now. We shall never forget him, nor will
the passage of the years ever dim out our love for this 'Verray parfit,
gentil knyght.'

A traveller from Naini Tal took the news to his hometown,
Kaladhungi, on the evening of 22 April. In true Hindu tradition the children were fed on the leftovers and the hearths were

left cold at night in Choti Haldwani. When a near and dear one goes, a meal is skipped. The news also laid to rest a story current for years that he had been devoured by an African lion. (That was supposed to have happened after he had an accident when photographing lions.)

By the end of the next week local weeklies had spread the news to the remotest villages of Kumaon. There were tears for the benefactor in the areas infested by maneaters. When the largesse was distributed, he was remembered again.

B.M. Cornelius, a friend, writing in the Delhi edition of the *Statesman* of 30 April 1955, suggested that a statue be erected in Corbett's memory at Naini Tal by public subscription. He wrote: 'The news of Col. Jim Corbett's death in Kenya is a reminder of a life of self-sacrifice and service. The people of the Kumaon region in particular will gratefully recall his courage and determination in tracking maneaters down and destroying them. . . . Corbett's name was a magic word of comfort to the people, and his presence brought reassurance and peace in the panic-stricken hills. . . . Now that he is dead, is it enough to say "How sad!" Would it not be in the fitness of things to raise a monument to his memory? I would suggest that funds be raised to set up a life-size statue of him at Naini Tal, which will recall to the people a life of noble service.'

Did Corbett ever want to return home to India? In 1948, the ties were fresh. A letter he wrote from Nyeri to Ram Datt Sati, who owned a cloth shop in the Kaladhungi bazaar, asked about the state of the mustard crop and hoped it had not been damaged by hail. 'Is the lorry service running between Haldwani and Ramnagar?' Corbett asks next. The service runs through Kaladhungi, the halfway point.

The letter reads: 'Has Ram Singh built his shop on the ground I gave him? Tell Ram Singh that when I come, I will expect to find my house and garden in good condition. Tell my assamis [tenants] that I am still with them and they are not to be anxious about anything. Both Miss Sahib [Maggie] and I are better now and when we are quite well, we will go back to our home in Kaladhungi.' Alas, that was not to be.

According to Naini Tal legend, Corbett buried his firearms in the grounds of Gurney House for a subsequent return. Jagat Singh was the only one who was supposed to know where the cache was.

If he had returned it would have been a hero's return. True, there would have been a few raised eyebrows (local Congressmen mostly), but to those to whom he mattered, the people of Kumaon and his village, he would have come back with the whole Corbett legend unimpaired with the passage of time. And what couldn't he have done for Indian wildlife? If he had stayed on, or come back, perhaps the near-ecocide of Stripes would have been averted.

At least once he was serious about a visit to the old country. A letter he wrote to Jagat Singh on 15 July 1951 said: 'If I am well enough, I will come to India this winter and I will look to you to help me. If the Hailey Park is still in existence, I should like to go to Bijrani and Malani for a few days to try and take some photographs of Bhabar villages.' He perhaps wanted these for *Jungle Lore*, which he was writing then.

On 10 December 1950, he had written to Jagat Singh: 'I am still suffering from the malaria I contracted during the war, and for this reason have not been able to return to Kumaon as soon as I had hoped for.'

Corbett was critical of the way the country was run after the departure of the British. He was not sure that Hailey National Park would be allowed to exist. He kept abreast of the developments in India—'I listen in every day to the broadcasts from Delhi.' He had doubted the success of the Tarai land reclamation project and compared it to the Kenya groundnut fiasco. He had his own sweeping solutions for the problems of the country. Writing to Jagat Singh, he observed: 'If I were the dictator of India, the first thing I would do would be to give the cultivators—who form 90 per cent of the population—security of life and property, and I would then shoot every man convicted of hoarding and blackmarketing.'

Then, in another context, he wrote: 'The ambition of three men to make a name for themselves has brought untold misery to millions of poor and innocent people and it is to be hoped that they will receive the punishment they deserve in the next world. Bad as her condition is today, it will get a hundred times worse when the red hand that is stretching down from the north gets the wounded country in her grip.' The red hand no doubt refers to the Soviet Union. It is not certain who the three men he referred to were. They could be the three dictators in power at the start of World War II.

13 The Wills

CORBETT AND Maggie both drafted their wills on 21 May 1954. Whether this was because of the uncertainty created by the Mau Mau uprising in the colony or Corbett's continued bad health we do not know. Though Maggie survived her brother by seven years she thought it unnecessary to revise her will.

A tremendous amount of family loyalty marks the bequests in Corbett's will. Sister Maggie was bequeathed all the income from his estate in her lifetime and the right to manage it and sell whatever she wanted, subject to a dozen other legacies made to several institutions and the Corbett clan distributed all over the globe.

The nearest relation, Douglas Corbett, of No 29 Victoria Road, New Barnet, Hertford, England, a nephew, was given 'the original manuscripts of all books written by me, my painted glazed miniature and my medals now held in safe custody by the Bank [The Standard Bank of South Africa Ltd., Nairobi, the executors of his will] with the request that they be retained in the Corbett family.' Douglas and his wife Saidi also got £1,000. The medals are a massive bunch. They could not possibly all be Corbett's. Maybe some were his father's.

We have already noted that Geoffrey Cumberlege, the Publisher of Oxford University Press, London, got a carpet. It measured eight feet by seven and was 'made in India over 100 years ago'. It was given to Cumberlege as a token of 'my affection and regard for all his kindness to my said sister [Maggie] and to myself'. This was the larger of the two carpets mentioned in the will and occupied Corbett's bedroom in Outspan Hotel, Nyeri. The smaller one was bequeathed 'unto my good friend, R.E. Hawkins, General Manager of the OUP in India, as a token of the same', along with nine volumes of his illustrated Shakespeare. The carpet, a Shiraz, measures nine feet by five. Henry Z. Walck, president, OUP, New York, was bequeathed the Bachelor of Powalgarh tiger skin. The will had elaborate instructions for the executors that the bequests should be properly packed and sent to the beneficiaries in tinlined cases.

Cumberlege met Corbett and Maggie in London and so did Hawkins. Hawkins also visited Maggie at Nyeri in 1962. As we have already noted, Walck did not get the Bachelor of Powalgarh. The fact that he had been mentioned in the will was a surprise to him. After Corbett's death Maggie wrote to him that, as the skin was not in prime condition, would he agree to have the Thak skin instead? Walck agreed. The skin is still with him.

Walck, who left OUP and then headed his own publishing firm in New York, was kind enough to supply me with details on his association with the hunter. 'I did not know Jim Corbett except through correspondence', he wrote. 'Several times we made tentative plans to meet in New York or London but unfortunately we were never able to carry through. We got best acquainted, I suppose, because of income taxes. There was a complication: Jim Corbett was a British subject and for some reason this resulted in double taxation on all his income from the United States. I was finally successful in correcting this and we did receive a substantial rebate plus interest for him.'

The whereabouts of the Bachelor and other tiger skins is still a mystery. Did Maggie withhold the Bachelor to keep it with her for some sentimental reason? Corbett's tiger skins and other trophies were auctioned under his will by his executors. The bank has kept no records of the sale.

Many causes benefited under the will. He gave £500 for a playground at Nyeri for the use of all races. The Nairobi branch of the Salvation Army and St Dunstan's Institute got

£200 each. The Mount Kenya Hospital at Nyeri was given £200. The Boy Scouts Association and Girl Guides Association of Kenya both received £100 each. A similar sum went to St Cuthbert's Church at Nyeri for its repairs.

The other beneficiaries were of the Corbett clan, most of them nephews and nieces. Such clothing 'as he may care to have' went to Col Jeffrey Lincoln-Gordon, a niece's husband, of Maragua Fort Hall, Kenya, and the pictures and books (other than the collection left at Gurney House) to Gen. Thomas William Corbett of Mweiga, Kenya. The general's daughter Priscilla was to get £500 on attaining the age of twenty-one. A nephew, Ray Nestor, and his wife Dorothy, of London, got £1,000. Another nephew, St Elmo Haslett of the China Coast Officers Club, Hong Kong, was gifted a similar sum.

A legacy of £1,000 went to David Woodward of Cape Town in 'gratitude for his kindness to my brother John and his wife, Kathleen'. Tracking people from old addresses after seventeen years can be quite trying. I wrote to the address provided in the will to get particulars from the recipient, but there was no reply.

Remembering the twenty hours at Tree Tops with Princess Elizabeth and Prince Philip two years earlier, Corbett mentioned the Prince in the will. Clause 21 reads: 'Unto His Royal Highness the Duke of Edinburgh for the Playing Fields Association of England the sum of one thousand pounds sterling which with my respectful loyalty I beg that His Royal Highness will be graciously pleased to accept as a token of my gratitude for the kindness shown to me by Her Majesty the Queen and His Royal Highness at Tree Tops, Nyeri, aforesaid.'

A blind grandnephew, George Marshall, got £1,000 'to enable him to further his studies at the school for the blind'. Dorothy Lincoln-Gordon and her husband got an annuity purchased for £1,000. Another niece, Vivian Stutchbury of Surrey, England, got an annuity costing £500.

The royalties from all his books and other income accruing

after his death were bequeathed in equal proportion to St Dunstan's Institute for the Blind, No. 1 South Audley Street, London, George Marshall, and the private charities of Oxford University Press. The last enabled OUP India to start a fund for its staff, from which they could seek loans in emergencies.

The residue was bequeathed to all his grandnephews and grandnieces and the children of his nephew Douglas Corbett after the death of Maggie.

Maggie willed her fur coat 'and such of my clothing, linen and ornaments as she may care to have, to my niece Dorothy Lincoln-Gordon'. The pictures and the books went to Gen. Corbett. The residue of the estate was bequeathed 'unto my brother, Edward James Corbett, provided he shall survive me and in the event of his predeceasing me then I give, devise and bequeath the same unto his estate to the intent that the same shall fall into and become part of the estate for distribution accordingly.'

A reward for loyalty was quite in the Corbett tradition. The first codicil to the will drawn up on 26 February 1957 gave 5,000 shillings to Karlo Wagathuku, Maggie's African car driver, 'as an expression of the appreciation of my late brother Edward James Corbett and myself of his loyal service to us both.' The second codicil of 27 July 1959 records the transfer of the money. Karlo was not in Maggie's employment then.

After Kenya became free in 1963, the ex-India Whites made another exodus, this time to South Africa. Maggie died the same year. Lieut.-Gen. Corbett went to England.

The Duke of Edinburgh presided at the liquidation of this part of the empire (Kenya) and I wonder whether Corbett, had he been alive, would have remained the staunch loyalist he was when he mentioned the Duke in his will. Also at the midnight ceremony of 11–12 December 1963, when the Union Jack was lowered, among those present were generals of the Mau Mau. But by that time the Great White Lord in Kenya (*Bwana Mkubwa*) had become the Goddam White Man (*Mzungu*).

14 The Memorials

In the whole of this wonderful orbit
There will never be a second Jim Corbett
For his shikar fame and name
Will remain just the same
And to the end of time
As Jim Corbett.[1]

CORBETT DID not live to see India, his Old Country, confer on him in 1957 the signal honour of renaming its first national park after him.

The difference between a national park and a sanctuary is that the first is set up under legislative authority for all time to come while the second is set up under an executive order with variable permanency.

The London Wildlife Convention of 1933 defined a national park as an area '(a) placed under public control, the boundaries of which shall not be altered or any portion be capable of alienation except by the competent legislative authority, (b) set aside for the propagation, protection and preservation of wild animal life and wild vegetation and for the preservation of objects of aesthetic, geological, prehistoric, historical, archaeological or other scientific interest, for the benefit, advantage and enjoyment of the general public, and (c) in which the hunting, killing or capturing of fauna and the destruction or collection of flora is prohibited except by or under the direction or control of the park authorities.'

The conference acted as a primer to UP conservationists.

[1] Naini Tal schoolgirl verse.

But I don't know whether much sentiment for wildlife and its preservation was involved when the pioneers thought of starting a sanctuary south of the Ramganga in the Kalagarh and Ramnagar Forest Divisions. For the reserve, covering 323·75 square kilometres of foothill country, which later became a sanctuary and finally a national park, was fully girdled with shooting blocks. It was clear that the pioneers, Corbett for one, primarily wanted an area where the tiger would breed and multiply and stock the shooting blocks for ever.

The area absorbing the whole of the Dhara and part of the Malani and South Patli Dun shooting blocks selected for the reserve was well known to early hunters and also to anglers, Linlithgow for one. Patli Dun is the fifteen-mile-long valley of the Ramganga. It has wide terraces under grass and is famed for its jungle spring.

It is a riot of colour in April with the red of dhak in bloom, the mauve and purple of bauhinia, the green of shisham and yellow-and-gold of sal under new leaf. In May, the yellow amaltas sprigs cascade down the hillsides. The grass terraces teem with herbivora—sambar, chital, hog deer and pig. The undulating area has bear and gural, and elephants and tigers roam freely. The river provides the world's best mahseer fishing and has both varieties of crocodile. It has otters too.

The pioneers of the national park movement in UP were two forest officers, E.R. Stevens and E.A. Smythies. When Divisional Forest Officer of Ramnagar Forest Division, as early as 1916 Stevens had suggested that a sanctuary be started in the area. Smythies, who succeeded Stevens, backed the proposal in 1917, but it was rejected by Percy Wyndham, the Commissioner. One can well understand a tiger slayer's viewpoint. Sixteen years later, under the patronage of Hailey, the Society for the Preservation of Game in UP resuscitated the project, and the Forest Department was asked in 1933 to demarcate an area for a national park. Luckily, Smythies was still there as Conservator of Forests. Hailey asked him to make a proposal for a game sanctuary. To start with, a reserve was created because legislation would take time. In

1934, the Governor designated the area a sanctuary for five years, with a ban on all hunting. With the passing of the UP National Parks Bill by the province's Legislative Council in 1935, the sanctuary was upgraded into a national park and named after Hailey, and it was this park that was renamed after Corbett in 1957. New boundaries were fixed in 1940. Corbett knew Smythies well, for he writes of fixing a machan for Mrs Smythies over a cow killed by a tiger near his house at Kaladhungi. The forest officer was touring and had dropped in on the Corbetts for a cup of tea.

With the completion of the Ramganga dam at Kalagarh in June 1974 the park lost 46·6 square kilometres of land along the river terraces. To provide a bigger habitat for the tiger and to compensate for the loss of land from flooding, the park has now been extended to 528·8 square kilometres.

According to Corbett, when Hailey left UP the district officials 'combined and reduced the area of the park from 180 to 125 square miles'.[2] He wrote thus to E.P. Gee, two months before his own death while commenting on Gee's article, 'The Tigers of the Hailey National Park', in the Sunday *Statesman* of 19 October 1954. The cutting had been sent to Corbett by Stockley among others. Gee was in Kenya visiting the national parks there in October 1954, but he could not meet Corbett. Gee never met Stockley either, though they often wrote to each other. Stockley, who retired to Kenya, died there in 1955.

After reading the article, Corbett wrote to Hailey reminding him of a day's fishing in the Ramganga in which from one stand Hailey caught eighteen big ones and he, lower down, twelve. It took three men to carry the catch to the camping site.

The park was also the favourite studio of F.W. Champion of the Indian Forest Service. Most of the photographs of tigers in his two books were taken here. In later years Champion

[2] E.P. Gee, *The Wild Life of India.*

found animal photography so easy in Africa that he longed for the Indian tiger forest.

I followed Gee into Corbett National Park (then Hailey National Park) in May 1954 on a permit from the Forest Department. I stayed two nights at the Bijrani forest rest-house, in the Ramnagar Forest Division, and two nights each at the rest-houses of Sarapduli and Paterpani in the Kalagarh Forest Division. At Bijrani, the nightjars were vociferous at night under a waxing moon, and the rest-house compound resounded with their hammer-on-wood calls. In the afternoon, I saw three sambar hinds crossing a ridge overlooking Ratta Pani Rau. (*Rau* means a stream.) A blind with an observation post in a tree provided some excellent cover to watch chital feeding on the other side.

Sarapduli, which literally means 'snake's hole' in Garhwali, provided the quietest sanctuary for the fugitive from the city, with a murmuring river and the vesper song of the Himalayan thrush. Deer and peafowl called at night. By the river were week-old droppings of wild elephants.

Dhikala, the showpiece of the park which draws most of the tourist traffic now with its rest-house suites, hutments and annexe suites, is further down the river over a terrace with a backdrop of rolling hills to the north. Corbett frequently visited the place with Linlithgow and Hailey. I went over the visitor's book at the rest-house and read Linlithgow's remark after he caught a 36½-pound mahseer. 'A place of proved desire and known delight', he wrote. 'Met tiger in broad daylight', wrote another visitor.

The visitor's book had a very enlightening entry about a Divisional Forest Officer being on the mat for mistakenly shooting a tiger within the boundary of the park. The Conservator of Forests thought it fit to reprimand the errant officer in the visitor's book, which was open to the public.

Below the Sarapduli ford is Champion Pool, named after the photographer of tigers. The road from the rest-house to the pool was under waist-high scrub. Apparently angling was not much in fashion after the departure of the British.

Patli Dun begins at Sarapduli and ends below at Boxar. The flowering cycle starts with the blood-red flowers of the silk cotton, followed by the scarlet-and-orange of dhak, and ends with amaltas. Nearer ground level, the star-shaped karonda flowers release a heady bouquet.

Ornithologically, Sarapduli was interesting, with a pair of mating rollers and the din raised by a school of hawk cuckoos. I particularly remember a hoarse-throated one which exercised its vocal chords far into the night.

After a memorable lunch, made so because of a welcome change provided by wild figs (collected at the Sitabani fresh-water swamp) from the eternal potato and onion—conditions were rather primitive then—I drove to Dhikala at dusk to meet Ramanand Gairola, Divisional Forest Officer of Kala-garh and a friend. He was away on his elephant on inspection when I arrived, so I drove to the edge of the forest to an observation post in a tree. I saw no wildlife in the hour I spent there, except for the imprint of four oily bear paws and of an equally oily posterior on the boards of the platform. When Gairola returned, I spent an hour with him discussing the park and the experiments he was conducting with an artificial saltlick there. I drove back for the night to Sarapduli.

I was advised to take a motorable stretch of road from Dhikala to Paterpani. Called Sambar Road, it hugged the forest all the way and provided some fine moments, deer and pig blocking the road at an early hour and disputing our right of way. When the right was unwillingly given, we were kept under watch. For some inexplicable reason the park deer seemed to tolerate cars but not the pedestrians. When we got out, the pig and chital bolted for cover.

Paterpani is on a knoll. The keeper of the rest-house was away and the driver of our borrowed vintage Chevrolet, an excellent mechanic, showed his prowess as a housebreaker without leaving a single scratch on the door. I received a pail of milk from Boxar through the hospitality of the Forest Department at noon, with a note that the keeper would be there before sundown, and he was.

I had expected to see much jungle life at Paterpani because of its location deep inside the park, but my luck was out. The next day a forest fire began, perhaps started by cameleers whom we had heard at night carrying bhabar grass to the paper mill depot at Kalagarh. It raged for three days. All wildlife vanished. A plucky junior forest officer with a truckload of men was all the Forest Department could muster to put it out.

I did not go to the point there, with 'the best view in the Western Circle', and instead devoted a whole evening to Paterpani Rau, reading the tracks on the sand. All of them were there—some recent, some old—tiger, bear, deer, elephant and python. Two black partridges fought on the sand, and a peacock strutted, all fanned out, before his hen. Here, I also met the first ant-lion of the park. The swamp at the base of the knoll provided some young shoots of fern for dinner.

Gee was luckier at Paterpani. He shot a long movie on a tiger scrutinizing him from tall elephant grass. The tiger, a biggish one, moved, and Gee, making a detour, stopped it and photographed it for a full five minutes. If someone on the elephant he was travelling on had not coughed, the tiger would have given him more time.

Because of the peculiar hydrography of the park—all the streams flow either north or south—it is inaccessible between June and October. The roads and temporary bridges are ready generally by the middle of December. April is the ideal month for a visit. The jungle spring is on and the new grass on the river flats is low. The animals can be seen better.

Apart from the accommodation provided at Dhikala for the tourist, there are several forest rest-houses within the park or along its periphery for the keen naturalist. They are at Sultan, Sarapduli, Boxar, Paterpani, Gaujpani, Jamnagwar, Bijrani, Malani, Mohan, Kanda, Gairal and Kalagarh. One can stay in any of them on a permit from the Forest Department if they are unoccupied by touring forest officers.

Much has to be done here if Stripes is to be saved. The

forestry operations should have been stopped, but they have not been and at one time every 'contractor's lorry carried a gun'.[3] The forestry operations disturb wildlife and the ecological balance. Cattle, allowed to graze within the park, have started rinderpest and hoof-and-mouth epidemics with considerable fatalities among the park's deer. They have now been removed.

The park was in the limelight on 1 April 1973 when the Government of India chose it to launch Project Tiger, a big effort to save Stripes from extinction. A general ban on tiger shooting had come in 1971.

Conscious of the urgency of the situation, the Indian Board for Wild Life dislodged the lion as the national animal, an honour it had enjoyed since 1967, and installed *Panthera tigris* in its place on 18 November 1972. The lion had been protected since 1958.

The project was started not a day too soon, for on that day the all-India tiger count, based on pugmarks, stood at 1,827. In Corbett Park itself their number had dwindled in three years from 74 to 46. It was estimated that in recent years India had been losing 100 tigers a year.

Corbett fans expected much at his centenary celebrations starting on 25 July 1975. The papers and magazines did rise to the occasion with articles, but the Government of India chose not to issue a centenary stamp even on the due date, in spite of declaring that it would do so. Finally, the Pandit Pant Memorial Committee managed to get the stamp released on 24 January 1976. And what a stamp! It showed a tiger, not a portrait of Corbett.

The idea of acquiring Corbett's house at Kaladhungi for a museum was first mooted in 1964 at a meeting of forest officers with the Forest Minister of UP at Dhikala. Seeing the building's dilapidated condition, admirers of the hunter appealed to the government to save it. Its new owner struck

[3] E.P. Gee, *The Wild Life of India.*

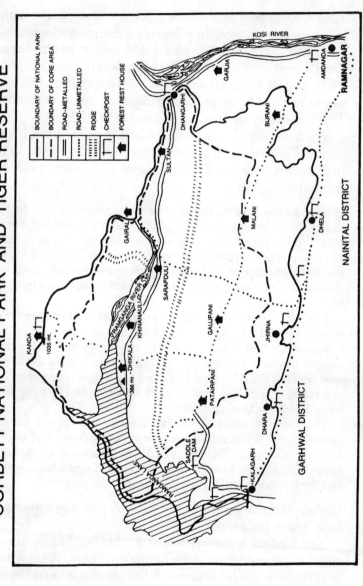

CORBETT NATIONAL PARK AND TIGER RESERVE

KOSI RIVER

RAMNAGAR

AMDANDA

GARJIA

BURANI

DHANGARHI

SULTAN

MALANI

DHELA

NAINITAL DISTRICT

GAIRAL

SARAPDULI

RAMGANGA RIVER

KHINNANAULI

1035 mt.

KANDA

DHIKALA

386 mt.

GAUJPANI

JHIRNA

PATAIRPANI

DHARA

SADDLE DAM

DHARA

RAMGANGA LAKE

KALAGARH

GARHWAL DISTRICT

BOUNDARY OF NATIONAL PARK
BOUNDARY OF CORE AREA
ROAD - METALLED
ROAD - UNMETALLED
RIDGE
CHECKPOST
FOREST REST HOUSE

a hard bargain after vacillating for months. In 1965, the government even thought of legal proceedings for its acquisition. The owner finally yielded and sold it to the Forest Department for Rs 50,000. The house was repaired in 1966–7 at a cost of Rs 5,000 and a watchman installed. The idea was to keep the house as it was without changing its identity. The Forest Department has succeeded in doing so.

We have already noted that Corbett wanted the house back in his lifetime for a community centre. In a letter to its new owner, Chiranji Lal Sah, dated 13 January 1952, he wrote from Nyeri:

When I let you have the bungalow at Kaladhungi, I was under the impression that you were going to make it your winter home. Several other people were wanting the bungalow, but as you and all the members of your family were my friends, I decided to give you the preference to enable you to get out of the cold for a few months, and to have a man of standing in the village to whom the tenants could look for help in case of need.

I am afraid that things have not worked out as I had hoped they would and if I am right in thinking that you are finding the bungalow a white elephant, I will be very happy and very greatly obliged to you if you will give it back to me. The Rs 2,000 you gave me is in the Allahabad Bank and I will have it transferred to you together with any money you have spent on the bungalow, immediately on hearing from you.

You can rest assured I am not making this request for any personal gain. If you will let me have the bungalow, I will offer it as a free gift to the Premier [of UP] to be used as a panchayat house. Kaladhungi, I understand, is in need of a panchayat house, and the bungalow will be very suitable for this purpose.[4]

Corbett did not get the house back. A panchayat ghar was built nearer the bazaar.

The Corbett museum, housed in this building, is a poor effort at commemorating the hunter's memory. There are no trophies here, nor his firearms. A few photographs and letters hang on the walls, and a cupboard contains junk left by the

[4] Courtesy Corbett museum.

hunter or diligently collected from the village by the Forest Department: three wine glasses, a flask, two egg-cups, two trays for washing photographs, a vase, a tureen, a saw and three weights. A Dietz hurricane lantern sits over the fireplace. The photographs are of interest though, a family portrait, one of Corbett with a bird and another of him holding a record 50-pound mahseer he caught in Naini Tal lake.

This mahseer is still a lake record. Corbett caught it on very light tackle. The fish, for its weight, did not give much fight and Corbett wondered if it had been spawning or was unwell. A print of this picture hung for years in the Naini Tal Yacht Club, of which Corbett was a member. When Corbett left, the club members took it down and packed it for him at a farewell function. That was the best memento they could think of for the departing angler.

The museum house faces north. On clear days, one can see the temples of Hanumangarhi at Naini Tal from there. The museum is in two sections. As you face it, the section to the right houses the main museum. The left is the area which Corbett himself occupied; it has his folding steel camp cot and the gun rack which once held his armoury, the most-publicized of which were his ·275 rifle, a Westley Richards ·500 double-barrel express rifle, and a 28-bore shotgun. It now holds only his cracked walking stick. Outside, to the right, are the graves of his dogs, Roshina and Robin.

While the villagers rifled Corbett's belongings from the untenanted house after his departure for Africa, the townsmen had other ideas. After Corbett's death, pressing invitations went to Maggie to come and visit the place. She was even invited to attend the Krishna Lila celebrations. The ruins of Arundel were still there and the land with it to be disposed of, and the townsmen wrote to Maggie asking her to give the land to them to start a high school. Maggie agreed in 1958 to give away the land to found a Corbett Memorial High School. The townsmen collected Rs 33,000 for the project. But politics stepped in. The town split into two—Corbett fans and Anglophobes. The second group protested that they would not have an institution named after a Briton.

Belatedly, Kaladhungi got its high school in the centenary year by upgrading the junior high school which functions at the panchayat ghar. It has happily been named Corbett High School. And the land, gifted for a worthy cause, has been appropriated by two townsmen and turned into a farm. Except for a lone wall, there is no trace of the old house now. Maggie gifted another stretch of land to the Forest Department in 1961. But credit goes to the people of Naini Tal who, with their meagre resources, managed to publish a souvenir to mark Corbett's centenary and launch a society, called the Fauna and Flora Preservation Society of India, in memory of him. A high-altitude zoo in now functioning. The UP government was persuaded to name the Naini Tal–Kaladhungi road Jim Corbett Road and the railways to rename the triweekly Kathgodam-Lucknow Express after the hunter-naturalist.

As I close this book—I hope it isn't a hagiography in spite of my unbounded admiration for the man—nearly four decades after his death, Corbett remains an ageless legend to kindle the hearts of each new generation to acts of courage and high adventure, even when few living men see a tiger outside a zoo cage. The legend will outlive the tiger whom he called a 'large-hearted gentleman with boundless courage'. And all will agree that he, too, was one. Starting the universal journey to the happy hunting grounds, his last words to his sister, 'Make the world a happy place for other people to live in', pithily embodied his philosophy of life, and he stuck to it stoically through prosperity and adversity in equal measure.

Appendix

Poem of the Panther

(a transcreation by Col S.N. Dhondiyal of *Bag ki Kavita*, a Garhwali ballad printed in *Bir Gharhwal* (1972), published by Shri
Vishalmani Sharma Upadhyaya of Narayan Kothi, Garhwal)

It was terror, not the usual fun and banter
That forged a fair — this time to catch a panther.
In Patti Nagpur, year nineteen twenty-five
Plans were launched, and then a concerted drive,
To trap the killer once the harvest was done:
Now rejoice, good folk! Happy times have come.

The panther had killed daughters, daughters-in-law,
Maimed cattle, mangled a babe with its paw.
No one knew when and where it would appear,
Snatch away a person and then disappear.
The panther roamed near us, lurked all around,
We poisoned its drinking pools, laid traps on the ground;
We fortified houses, but the killer still killed —
Our voices went silent, in fear our blood chilled.

Nineteen eighteen's fever* was coupled with fear
Of a panther addicted to human blood-smear.
A child was devoured — 'Who next?' None could say;
From Bhattisera to Karnaprayag the killer held sway.

---

* The influenza epidemic that followed World War I

Patwaris gathered three hundred goats, as bait;
But we didn't see the panther, despite a long wait.
Came Captain Saurat* to Rudraprayag: he fired his gun
Near the bridge; the panther now wounded,
     was made to run.
But the maneater yet lived, survived bullets, poison;
Hunters arrived, and Chopra was garrisoned.
But the traps remained empty and the hunters though keen
Confessed six months later that the panther was unseen.

Then came Hariram Dhasmana, the good Tehsildar;
He worked out a plan to be executed like a war.
Searching for the maneater day and night, hail or rain
He traversed the mountains and their rocky terrain.
Commissioner Abbotson** was there to hold his hand
He summoned patti-dwellers, and many a brass band.
The tumult of the instruments echoed and filled
Forests; seventeen panthers emerged, they were soon killed.

But the maneating monster eluded all, roaming free;
Untraced, it continued with its vicious killing spree.
O Lord! Are there no Kshatriyas worthy of their name,
To do battle with the monster and earn righteous fame?
Ram defeated Ravan, Krishna uprooted evil;
God, come and save us, rid us of this devil.

---

* An officer of the Garhwal Rifles
** The local name for Ibbetson